START WITH RESPECT

A Principled Path for Leading Change

BILL POOLE

Author of *Journey to Newland*

PRAISE FOR
START WITH RESPECT

"In our time of unprecedented uncertainty when every organization is facing the need to transform and build lasting change agility, Bill has created a masterly and practical framework for leading organizational transformations."

—**ARINYA TALERNGSRI**, Founder and Managing Director, Southeast Asia Center (SEAC)

"Whether you're a first-time supervisor or a more seasoned leader, *Start with Respect* will prepare you to embrace change, both on a professional and a personal level. Bill Poole will engage you with his stories, intertwining respect, trust, and influence into a system that is simple to grasp, remember, and apply."

—**DR. JANELLE K. WARD**, Founder, BRIO Solutions

"Work in the nonprofit world, perhaps even more so than in other sectors, needs to be centered around respect because it involves serving and supporting individuals, communities, and causes for those who may be vulnerable or marginalized. Bill Poole's Start with Respect provides the guiderails we all need to serve others better."

—**BILL MAIKRANZ**, President and CEO, United Way of South Central Idaho

"You may have massive intelligence and talent, but like Bill Poole says in *Start with Respect*, if you don't start your work or relationships with respect, you won't finish well and achieve your desired results."

—**DAN MCCORMICK**, Direct Sales Consultant, Speaker and Author of *Awakening Who I Am*

"As we navigate the deep waters of relationships, we sometimes sink below the surface. Bill Poole has provided us with lifesaving wisdom. Respect is the common denominator of all healthy relationships."

—**TRES TANNER, PHD,** Relationships Expert, Entrepreneur, and Author of *Enjoy the Journey along Your Marriage Highway*

"I am often asked, 'How can I make my dreams come true?' Bill Poole gives us all a foolproof answer: Start with respect!"

—**ROB SPERRY**, Entrepreneur, Sales Leader, and Author of *Die with Memories, Not Dreams*

"As an experienced keynote speaker, I know what people respond to, what they resonate with, and that is love and respect. As my good friend Bev Kaye says, you either love them or you lose them. Bill Poole's book makes the point crystal clear: you either start with respect or end with regret. We need to show respect now more than ever!"

—**EILEEN McDARGH**, CEO, The Resiliency Group, Hall of Fame Speaker, and Author

"Having coached and judged thousands of amateur and professional dancers from around the world, we can agree with Bill Poole: You don't want to start off on the wrong foot or step on toes. To win championships and sustain partnerships and relationships, you must start with mutual respect."

—**LEE AND LINDA WAKEFIELD**, International Ballroom Dance Coaches, Judges, Choreographers, and Champions

"For the past 35 years, I have been deeply involved in starting and building several companies and in advising the leaders of organizations. And Bill Poole's book title rings true with me because how you start a business often determines how long you stay in business."

—SCOTT PETERSEN, CEO, Consultant, and Serial Entrepreneur

"In our quest to find our flow in work and life, we learn that building supportive, respectful, and trusting relationships is vital. In this book, Bill Poole illustrates how respect builds trust, and trust boosts influence, which leads to optimizing our engagement with others. Having coached and consulted with many elite performers and leaders, I see how building trust in ourselves and others facilitates collaborative partnerships and peak performance. Bill can help you find your flow."

—**BRUCE H. JACKSON, MBA/MPA, PhD**, Principal, Attentional Leadership Institute, and Author of *Finding Your Flow*

"Bill Poole brings the energy of Tony Robbins and the magic of Walt Disney to engage and inspire leaders to embrace the change capability mindset necessary to lead in today's complex world. *Start with Respect* will help you embrace the courage necessary to make respect a part of your career legacy."

—**KARA FORT**, President and CEO, 2 Serve Solutions Inc.

"Bill has simplified the uncompromising complexities in leadership, systems thinking and building a learning organization. *Start with Respect* unlocks people, both professionally AND personally.

—**DAVID BENNETT**, Director of Fleet Service, Equipment Depot

"The insurance industry is in a constant state of flux. Our clients rely on us to provide advice, guidance, and counsel during these times of uncertainty. As our company continues to evolve in this changing environment, our employees deserve the same type of direction and support. Bill Poole reminds us as leaders to focus on the principles that don't change—starting with respect."

—**NICOLE WISE**, Chief Operating Officer, Sentinel Risk Advisors

For additional copies/bulk purchases of this book please contact:
info@startwithrespect.com

ISBN 978-1-7330973-1-4

For more information on supporting content or services, please visit our website at startwithrespect.com.

This book is dedicated to my business partners
who consistently model these principles and
always treat me with the deepest respect:

Rick Cobb, J2N Global
Arinya Talerngsri, Southeast Asia Center
Winnie Wang, Visionary Consulting
Ken Shelton, Executive Excellence
Lisa Shannon, Big Sky Bold
Sean Cary and HD Interactive Team

• • •

In memory of my mentors who taught and
modeled these principles, and who are
smiling down from heaven shocked that I finally
got this book written: Bob Pettus,
Dr. Jerry McKinney, and Dick Jordan.

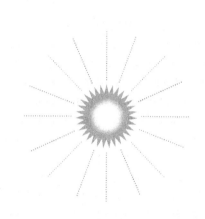

CONTENTS

INTRODUCTION

I'm concerned.

Uncertainty. Polarization. Anger. Apathy.

Sadly, these words describe what I see happening in our workplaces and in the broader culture.

I'm concerned about incivility and the lack of will for healing the conflicts and societal scars that only seem to get deeper and more dangerous.

I'm concerned about our digital tools and platforms. While many of these innovations have positively transformed our world, they have also damaged how people relate to one another.

I'm concerned that it has become difficult to discern the truth. Our news feeds are stuffed with shallow and biased sources that perpetuate lies and half-truths for the sake of ratings and dopamine clicks.

I'm concerned that we can't trust our institutions because of the flawed systems and corrupt leaders who control them.

I'm concerned that respect gets no respect, and that disrespect gets applauded and rewarded.

And I'm concerned for the wise, capable leaders in our organizations who are beyond frustrated with the unhealthy cultures and systems that they can't seem to change.

I wrote this book for those leaders. If you are one of those leaders, I encourage you to use this book as a roadmap for transformational change.

RAYS OF LIGHT

Yes, I'm concerned, but I'm also hopeful because the darker it gets, the brighter the rays of light will shine.

I'm hopeful because I believe unchangeable human principles will prevail.

I'm hopeful because I see many good leaders ready to rise to the challenge.

I'm hopeful because I know that deep down, we all want to be respected. During my graduate work, I studied the major religions. I found that they all teach the universal importance of respect. Respect is central to the human condition. Respect appeals to our higher nature.

I'm hopeful because I've seen how starting with respect can transform people, teams, and organizations.

WHY WE NEED TO START WITH RESPECT

When people ask me why I'm adamant about starting with respect when facing transformational change, I often tell them about my conversation with Daryl Holt.

Daryl's call for help came out of the blue. He was an executive at a major video game development studio for one of the largest interactive entertainment publishers in the world, and we had previously worked together. He was familiar with my methods. The problem, as he saw it, was that a lack of trust across various levels and disciplines was stifling creativity and execution in his organization. The studio had grown rapidly, doubling in size multiple times over the previous three years. He asked me if I could do a session on trust building.

I responded with a question. "Can you put two people in a room and demand that they trust each other?"

Daryl gave it a quick thought and said, "No, I don't think that would work."

We agreed that if you order two people to trust each other, it will backfire. It will work against the principle of trust—especially if they have legitimate reasons not to trust each other. The intention might be a good one, but it would have the opposite effect.

I continued, "Okay, so can you put the same two people in a room and demand they show respect for each other? Keep in mind, they don't need to actually have respect for each other; they just have to show it, assuming you have clearly defined what showing respect looks like."

He quickly agreed with my assertion, so I continued. "Would holding people accountable to show respect be a good first step toward establishing trust?"

"Absolutely!" he responded.

We discussed the start-with-respect-to-get-to-trust concept. Once trust and credibility are established, we observed, one natural outcome is to have mutual influence up, down, and across the organization. Paradoxically, the optimal way to get to trust is not to start with trust but to start with respect. Any other path would focus on the symptom, putting a Band-Aid on the real problem. Daryl had big plans for his studio, so he was anxious to get rolling. He confided that developing trust was just the first step. He wanted to create a leadership culture that could respond to disruption and uncertainty, creating unmatched transformational change capability.

"Let's go," I said.

> The optimal way to get to trust is not to start with trust but to start with respect.

*We are destined to run into glass walls
when we do what comes natural and normal.*

NORMAL VERSUS OPTIMAL

How would you describe your business environment? What is it like to be a leader in your team or organization?

Are you at the helm of a beautiful, sturdy sailboat? The ocean waters are calm. A slight breeze fills the sails, gently propelling you and your crew to the desired destination. The sun shines brightly—not a cloud in the sky. You can see for miles.

Or are you grappling with a boat that has been blown off course by an unexpected storm? A gale-force wind and ocean swells repeatedly knock you to the floor. Your crew is at odds, unable to agree on the best way to navigate the storm. As the rain pelts your face, you suddenly realize that poor visibility has hidden a rocky jetty. You are about to crash!

For many, the second scenario is a more accurate picture of what it's like to be a leader in today's business environment.

Disruption. Uncertainty. Polarization. This is the world of leaders today. Complex challenges stack up by the day. And while many leaders come to work each day with a noble ambition to build a better organization and to make a positive impact on people's lives and their company's bottom line, they are often stymied by failed efforts to lead change.

Here's the truth: either we learn to lead change, or change leads us. And here's the paradox: the best way to lead change is to focus on principles that don't change.

> The best way to lead change is to focus on principles that don't change.

So how do we create healthy cultures and lead authentic and sustainable change? I believe it starts with respect!

THE NATURAL DEFAULT

When the winds of change blow our way, we often default to doing what comes naturally, what feels normal. In many contexts, *natural* and *normal* serve us well. It's a very human inclination to rely on our intuition or habit when trying to make the best decision and solve the problems in front of us. However, amid the complexities of change, *natural* and *normal* will often derail leaders. To lead change effectively, we must do what's *optimal*.

The normal and natural path to leading change in our uncertain and polarized world looks quick and easy since it's been beaten down by the footsteps of people who previously traveled the same path. It's the path dictated by the technological algorithms for reinforcing our assumptions and appealing to our comfort zone. Most people who travel this easy path don't consider that they are merely following others who followed others who followed others. "That's the way we do it here" is their refrain. The path looks clear, well-worn, and wide open, so we assume this normal path is the best path. However, the normal path often takes us deeper into polarization by appealing to what we already believe, reinforcing our ingrained assumptions and reigniting the flames of anger.

> The normal path often takes us deeper into polarization by appealing to what we already believe.

GLASS WALLS

People and organizations that do what comes naturally by default are destined to run into glass walls. It's like the old Windex commercial where two birds clean a man's sliding door with Windex and then sit in a tree to watch the man walk into his sliding door and fall flat on his back because the wall of glass is so clean and clear, he can't see it. The bantering birds chuckle and say, "Let's do it again!"

In complex change situations, we are destined to run into glass walls when we do what seems natural and normal. You know the drill. A deadline is looming, or it is almost the end of the quarter. We focus on tangible results. It's natural. Or the merger happens. The chiefs run the numbers, ink the deal, and exit the boardroom slapping high fives. The people part will be easy. Then, as they start the transition, they smash into glass walls. The broken glass rains down on everyone involved.

Glass walls can't be seen when you ignore the optimal.

AN OPTIMAL PATH TO CHANGE

This book is about transformational change capability. In the following chapters I introduce an alternative change path, an optimal path. It's a path that starts with respect. It's for those who are tired of the normal path of disrespect, fear, manipulation, and control. This optimal path is better suited for our transformational change journeys. When taking this path, you will inevitably splash some dirt on the systems that act as glass walls. Systems are complex and hard to see at times, but not seeing them, not changing them, will leave you flat on your face. This path is the key to leading your teams and organizations through the difficulties of transformational change.

FROM *JOURNEY TO NEWLAND* TO RESPECT, TRUST, AND INFLUENCE

Several years ago I wrote a book titled *Journey to Newland: A Road Map for Transformational Change.* It's an allegory that features a cast of animated characters facing a major change. These characters realize that to survive and prosper, they must leave familiar territory and natural ways in Oldland and venture to find what's optimal in Newland.

The underlying principles in that book are universal in their applications and highly relevant to today's conditions. The main takeaway of the *Journey to Newland* story is this: when leading change and overcoming resistance, it is always optimal to start with respect.

I find that this simple yet profound progression—from *respect* to *trust* to *influence* (the RTI path and model)—resonates with people all around the globe. This, then, is the treatise for my work with leaders and organizations: the optimal path to leading positive change in our uncertain and polarized world starts with respect.

> ## The optimal path to leading positive change starts with respect.

Journey to Newland focused on the characters and the map in a business fable. This book describes in detail the principled path to leading change. This *respect* to *trust* to *influence* model is presented on the following page. I call it the RTI path.

THE RTI PATH™

RESPECT

1 **SUSPEND ASSUMPTIONS**
Identify and challenge deep-seated mental models, perspectives, and paradigms.

2 **VALUE DIFFERENCES**
Avoid accidental adversaries and generate multi-level and cross-functional collaboration to create and fix systems, solve root problems, and make optimal decisions.

TRUST

3 **CULTIVATE OPENNESS**
Create an environment of truth and authenticity over politics and fear.

4 **EXPAND DIALOGUE**
Master a versatile dialogue tool for conversation, facilitation, innovation, negotiation, or mediation that leads to optimal options.

INFLUENCE

5 **HONOR BOUNDARIES**
Leverage respect to balance results and relationships through appropriate leadership and communication styles.

6 **CREATE LEADERS**
Focus on creating leaders up and down and across the organization. Build a leadership culture that attracts, retains, develops, aligns, and promotes leaders at all levels of the organization to grow, produce, and reproduce in a sustainable system.

The journey through uncertainty and polarization requires us to seek a new mindset and paradigm when following the RTI path toward transformational change.

Interested in diving deeper into
Normal versus Optimal?

Download more resources and tools at
startwithrespect.com.

Are you leading change, or is change leading you?

A NEW CHANGE
CAPABILITY MINDSET

For a change initiative to be successful, leaders need to focus on mindset as much as skill set. The RTI path helps leaders create mindsets that make transition and transformation happen.

> For a change initiative to be successful, leaders need to focus on mindset as much as skill set.

I developed the change mindset model to help leaders understand people's typical behavior in change situations. The model also helps us become more aware of how we experience change and how others experience us during change. The four squares in the model represent four types of human responses to change: transformers, reactors, controllers, and resisters.

- **Transformers** influence others by leading change. Transformers are leaders who transform themselves while influencing others to transform. Transformers include innovators and early adopters.
- **Reactors** are good followers who are open to change and can be influenced by other change mindsets. They depend on others to initiate change. Their enthusiasm for change can range from being strongly positive to being strongly negative. Since they don't stay in the reactor quadrant once they are influenced by the other quadrants, you need to pull them into the transformer quadrant. Helping Reactors become Transformers is crucial to creating an early majority.
- **Controllers** may have positional or personal influence, but they are more concerned with image and territorial control

than with making transformational change. Controllers who
make the journey become the late majority.

- **Resisters** are unwilling to transform themselves or others.
  They are skeptical and fight any change that requires moving
  out of their comfort zone. Resisters who make the journey also
  become the late majority.

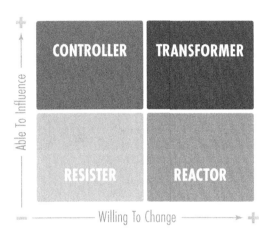

Where do you and your team members fit in this model?
What tendencies do you have? What qualities and capabilities are needed for a transformational change initiative to be
successful?

STUCK IN REACTOR MODE

When too many people get stuck in reactor mode, they can block transformational change initiatives. What does this look like? Reactors are waiting to be deployed instead of proactively moving into the transformer quadrant. When upstream transformers don't identify and develop downstream transformers, they must "move down" to make up for this leadership gap.

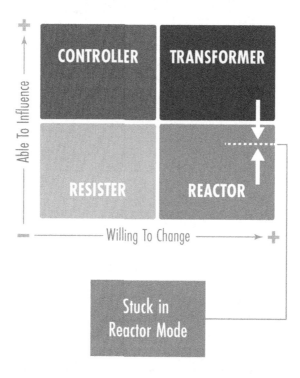

In the *Start with Respect* system, transformers use RTI to pull reactors into the transformer quadrant to create a leaders-of-leaders culture. Now transformers can move up the influence axis as well.

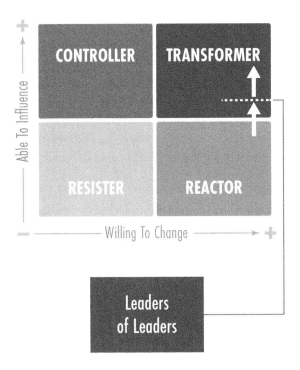

GETTING UNSTUCK WITH LEADERSHIP CAPABILITY

If your change capability is insufficient to anticipate or implement change, it will limit options for change. Leaders must not only create capability to respond to change, but they must also anticipate capacity. Change capability gives us bench strength, and change capacity gives us a broader bench. This is why a creating-leaders strategy is crucial.

Implementing the RTI model enables us to see opportunity or innovation potential in situations. It optimizes results and relationships and all other capabilities. It optimizes everyone and everything.

Since transformation requires transformers, the RTI strategy starts with a leadership team made of transformers to model the new system and create pull. Once we choose leaders with a respect mindset, we can confront and move out the leaders with a disrespect mindset. Thus, here is the secret for those who want to progress along the RTI path: Leaders must have the wisdom to choose and courage to confront. Everything starts with the mindset of the leader. The system and culture always follow.

> Leaders must have the wisdom to choose
> and courage to confront.

THE SUN AS A SOURCE

Optimal change capability is principle-centered, and principle-centered change capability is like the sun—it is self-sustaining and regenerating. You don't have to turn on the sun, and it never goes out. If it's behind the clouds or on the other side of the earth, it's still there. The intangible effects of the sun remain whether you see it or not. The sun is a constant source of light and heat. It is constantly regenerating and transforming itself into new energy. It is not dependent on the other planets, but it influences the other planets—how they move, how they align. It is central to our solar system.

As people, teams, and organizations, we want to be like the sun—self-sustaining and regenerating. We don't want to be always responding and oscillating. We want to create our future, not simply react to it. We want to be ready to reinvent ourselves, our teams, our organizations, and our businesses at any moment.

Being like the sun will help us burn off the fog and succeed on our transformation journey.

Behind the energy and power of the sun is the unseen atomic structure, composed of a nucleus of protons and neutrons surrounded by electrons.

RTI is like the atomic structure of principle-centered change capability. Respect and trust combine to form the nucleus. Influence acts like electrons, circling and interacting with the nucleus where the energy, movement, and results are felt in more tangible ways.

INTANGIBLE FORCES

● Respect ● Trust ● Influence

When RTI elements are built into the individual, team, or organization structure, they create six life-giving forces that can be tapped to lead and sustain change:

1. **Energy** (intangible forces, mindset, motivation, engagement, and ownership)
2. **Pull** (vs push)
3. **Alignment** (values, processes, talent)
4. **Atmosphere** (environment, culture)
5. **Light** (vision)
6. **Heat** (confronting disrespect and being assertive about values, vision, respect)

CHANGE VERSUS TRANSITION

A vital skill in change leadership is knowing the difference between *change* and *transition*.

Change is situational—it involves exchanging one situation or context for another. For example, I can change the way I do invoices, I can choose to use new software, or I can relocate my home to a new city. Change is also transactional and behavioral. You can get people to change their behavior and hold them accountable by observing performance and tangible results, but you cannot make them internalize the change. You must allow time and provide support to help them go through the emotions involved in the transition.

Transition is emotional and psychological. Transition starts with mindset and attitude. A transition begins when mindset and emotions respond to a situation: a new way of invoicing makes me feel less confident, fearful, or uncomfortable; the new software makes me feel uncertain or anxious; or the new home makes me feel sentimental and nostalgic for the old place.

My friend and mentor Dr. Jerry McKinney defines transition as "a psychological process that allows people the time to come to terms with the situational changes."

A good example of the difference between change and transition is when someone gets married. When you get married, your situation changes. But if you still have a "single mindset," you're going to have problems! Your mindset hasn't caught up to your situation. You haven't completed the transition. The marriage system simply won't work if you have a single mindset in a married situation.

We sometimes describe transition as the phase of being "in between," similar to the transition game in basketball. However, even at this stage, mindset matters. For example, suppose I grab the rebound when I'm on defense. The transition phase will not start until my mindset changes from defense to offense. If my mindset is still on defense when my situation is on offense, I won't make the transition. Even if you use the term *transition* to refer to the in-between phase, you need to remember that mindset still determines success or failure.

MINDSET TRIGGERS AND RESPECT

In transition, mindset is more important than skill set. If the mindset and awareness are not transformed, change efforts are doomed to fail. Desired behaviors and results are manifest downstream from mindset.

A trigger is something that prompts a mindset change. It is the moment when you decide to get married or divorced. Often, when the trigger happens, there is no going back.

Some triggers happen organically, but when you are leading change, you want to be proactive in creating triggers. The challenge of purposely generating triggers is that they are often personal, dynamic, unpredictable, and sometimes fragile. They are likely hidden, both from others and within the person themselves. The leader's job is to identify and leverage triggers.

In transition, mindset is more important than skill set.

CHANGE CAPABILITY

Many leaders try to manage something they can't manage—change. *Change capability* means we are always ready for change and disruption. It is natural to want to manage change as it comes at us, but it is optimal to build change capability and the capacity to both lead and manage change.

Even if we're ready for a hurricane, it is never easy to withstand one. But if we aren't ready when the hurricane arrives, we have little chance of surviving, much less thriving in the storm.

There's a fine line between change management and change capability. Change management may work in some instances, but you must gear up for every change, dealing each time with the people and forces that resist. That takes a lot of energy and resources. Change management is generally reactive in nature.

Change capability involves both managing and leading change as well as responding to and creating change. Similar to individual leaders, many organizations lack true change capability because they are simply trying to manage change. They are constantly chasing change like a dog chases its tail. We must have the ability and agility to create change and respond to change simultaneously—to run fast like a cheetah and still turn on a dime. That's change capability.

Change capability involves both managing and leading change as well as responding to and creating change.

To respect is to look again.

DEFINING RESPECT

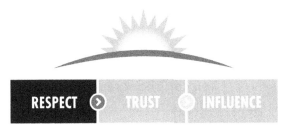

RESPECT ❯ TRUST ❯ INFLUENCE

Before we start our journey along the respect path, let's clarify what respect is, how it shows up, and how it impacts our lives.

The English word *respect* derives from Latin *respicere*, meaning "to look again." To look again is to refrain from judging a book by its cover—to see what's below the surface. When you show respect, you don't make snap judgments. This kind of looking and seeing connects to the formal definition of respect: to show high regard for someone or something.

HOW DOES RESPECT SHOW UP?

Respect shows up in several ways.

Respect is a principle at play in the universe since humanity began. When everything changes, respect stays the same. You can't hack respect. Like gravity, if you ignore it, you will crash. If you acknowledge it, it can help you soar. And since principles don't change, you can count on respect during times of uncertainty and change.

> You can't hack respect.

You can rely on respect when a situation can't be found in the corporate policy manual or instruction guide or in a best-selling self-help book. It can help you hire, fire, promote, and demote. It can guide you in almost every relationship and situation.

Like most principles, respect seems intangible but has tangible outcomes. Respect always has an influence, like the sun even when it's hiding behind the clouds. It's a constant in our environment.

Respect is an emotion. Most people don't think of respect as an emotion, but they definitely experience it this way. You have likely heard someone say, "I don't feel respected around here" or "I don't feel he respects me or what I do." That is respect showing up as an emotion.

Respect is a perception. Sometimes respect gets a bad rap since it's often a perception in one person's mind, not a fixed reality between two people. Since respect is a perception, it can be influenced by assumptions. It is often misunderstood, misused, misread, and misinterpreted. If you and another person are not on the same page regarding respect, your relationship will suffer. And without an intervention with respect at the center, those perceptions can spiral out of control.

Respect is a voice. Respect is your inner voice, self-talk, and conscience. If you never learned respect from your parents, teachers, or society, this voice may be faint and hard to hear. If you hear it and ignore it, your conscience can be seared, snuffed out, or crowded out; you may then lose an ear for respect, whether it whispers or shouts.

Respect is a choice. Respect sits on your shoulder like Jiminy Cricket advising Pinocchio, trying to get you to choose its path. It invites you to help yourself and others around you if you're open to hearing its voice. Respect's nemesis, disrespect, sits on your other shoulder shouting in your ear, trying to drown out the voice of respect. Disrespect has an advantage in the public square. It gets much more exposure in social media, politics, world affairs, movies, and songs. Disrespect is easy and quick. Respect is often difficult and demanding. It is not what the stock market, the bottom line, or peer pressure often demands from us in our daily lives.

Respect is dignity. As Christine Porath and Christine Pearson discuss in their *Harvard Business Review* article "The Price of Incivility," all humans are *owed* respect and dignity at a basic level, though additional respect can be *earned* by our interactions and behaviors. Respect shows dignity for others and appeals to our highest nature.

Respect is dynamic. Because respect is an emotion and a perception, it is dynamic. It may be here today but gone tomorrow with one action, one word or phrase, one glance, one gesture, one moment of apathy, one lack of response, one failure to acknowledge someone, one late arrival, or one slip of incongruent body language. Respect can change as fast as you can send or receive a text message.

Respect is a mindset. Respect is a paradigm, philosophy, mental model, and worldview. Respect is a lens through which we see life, make assumptions, make decisions, solve problems, and approach relationships. Your mindset toward respect determines not only your behavior and results but *how* you get results. In any organization, the mindset of the leader and the collective mindset toward respect will determine the culture.

> In any organization, the mindset of the leader and the collective mindset toward respect will determine the culture.

Respect is communication. When we are communicating with others, they can easily tell whether we have respect for them or not. They can sense it in our words, tone, and gestures. We can tell whether others respect us by how much time and focused attention they give us. We also can detect respect when they make the effort to tell us *why* rather than simply what, how, and when. This is the difference maker when leading change. Respect is the key to effective communication when we seek to optimize both relationships and results, not settling for one over the other.

Respect is a leadership style. Your mindset toward respect determines your leadership style. A respect mindset will help you lead through inclusion, input, participation, ownership, and mutual accountability. A smashmouth, my-way-or-the-highway leadership style comes from a mindset of disrespect where results trump respect, dollars trump dignity, and pride trumps humility. And when you're leading change, your leadership style will determine the success and the sustainability of the change you are leading.

THE RESPECT SEQUENCE

In the following chapters we will look at two elements of respect that form an optimal sequence for paving a path to trust and influence. The first step in the respect sequence is to *suspend assumptions*, which is based on the concept of "look again." Suspending assumptions is both the starting point and the leverage point when starting with respect. When we're leading change, if we assume others see what we see or assume we see what others see, we set ourselves up for failure from the start. To avoid this trap, we use this proven proposition to show how to start with

> Suspending assumptions is both the starting point and leverage point when starting with respect.

respect when leading change: *they won't see what you see until you see what they see.*

The second step in the respect sequence is to *value differences*. This requires us to suspend assumptions, listen optimally, win hearts and minds, and move people from simply agreeing to believing. When leading change, valuing differences increases engagement, input, participation, accountability, and trust. In an organization, it enables us to increase cross-functional collaboration, create and fix processes and systems, and communicate more effectively.

Now let's get started with how we suspend assumptions.

They won't see what you see until you see what they see.

SUSPEND ASSUMPTIONS

RESPECT 〉 TRUST ⬤ INFLUENCE

SUSPEND ASSUMPTIONS   CULTIVATE OPENNESS   HONOR BOUNDARIES
VALUE DIFFERENCES   EXPAND DIALOGUE   CREATE LEADERS

Come on! Don't just stand there!

Hey, you, up there! Get off your phone!

Pay attention! What a jerk!

Move it, you idiot!

These were the mumblings that escalated to shouts as I stepped from the jetway to the plane. As the line came to a standstill, I could see that the travelers in front of me were directing their ire at a woman standing in the aisle. She was about halfway toward the back of the plane. From my vantage point, it appeared as though no one was in front of her. Yet there she stood, oblivious to the impatient people behind her, slightly turned so that we could see her calmly typing on her phone.

Stopped dead in my tracks, a heavy backpack slung over my shoulder, and feeling worn out by a long workday, I was too tired to add to the heated cacophony aimed at this seemingly clueless woman. Instead, I groaned on the inside and stared at my feet.

After about a minute the verbal pokes came to a crescendo. A few alpha road warriors appeared ready to push their way through the line. I started to wonder if they would physically confront the woman. The flight attendants behind me looked nervous.

Then all at once a frail-looking elderly woman staggered up from the floor along with a frantic flight attendant. The elderly woman's luggage had gotten stuck when she tried to stuff it under her seat. The flight attendant had been working feverishly to help her unhitch her bag and clear the aisle for the ruthless crowd. The lady on the cell phone couldn't move forward, so she had been calmly texting while she waited.

The second these two women arose from the floor, you could hear a pin drop. The shouters in front of me immediately glanced at each other with sheepish grins and shrugs. A few looked down in shame. I watched it all in awe as the patient woman on the phone—the one who could see the full picture of what was happening in front of her—calmly made her way to the back of the plane and found her seat.

At best, flawed assumptions can make a temporary fool out of us. At worst, assumptions are the sparks that ignite the fires of many societal ills, including polarization and injustice, conflicts and wars, broken relationships, failed businesses, and poor health.

> Assumptions are the sparks that ignite the fires of many societal ills.

SNAPSHOTS

You probably remember that before our current era of smart phones and selfies, photographs were taken with a camera. A *snapshot* referred to a photo that was "shot" spontaneously and quickly, most often without artistic intent and with a cheap camera. Snapshots rendered memorable moments in imperfect images. They were often composed poorly and framed wrong, with out-of-focus subjects in bad light. The snapshot concept was popularized by Eastman Kodak's Brownie box camera in 1900. With the Brownie, you could capture "Kodak moments," quickly taking snapshots without being concerned about producing perfect images.

Like the impatient people in the plane, we often take amateur snapshots as we try to make sense of people and events unfolding around us. We might think we are capturing the whole story, when in truth we have an imperfect image, wrongly framed, outof focus, badly composed, or poorly lit. These snapshots tell a partial, prescribed, or prejudicial story.

CATCHING THE FULL MOVIE

Most of us make assumptions by looking at snapshots of the world around us. We catch glimpses of events and base our thinking on those glimpses. We naturally jump to conclusions based on these partial truths. Instead of relying on snapshots, leaders need to fill their perception gaps by catching the full movie. A movie fills in the frames between individual snapshots to give a fuller, truer picture of reality. We often draw false conclusions from snapshots and uncover corrected truths after seeing the movie.

When you understand the destructive significance of assumptions drawn from snapshots and can work toward suspending and challenging your assumptions, not only will you see the full picture with perspective, but you will also be more successful leading change.

SUSPEND AND CHALLENGE ASSUMPTIONS

My airplane experience illustrates what happens when people act after seeing only a snapshot of a situation. Assumptions lead to poor decisions that can lead to bad behavior. If the people waiting in the aisle had suspended their assumptions, if they had gathered more information from the flight attendants or observed the scene from a different angle, they would have been better equipped to make better decisions. They would have behaved better.

It's perfectly normal, perfectly human, to make assumptions. However, to demonstrate respect, we must practice suspending and challenging assumptions. We must make the intentional effort to look again.

RUNNING AT NIGHT

Before undergoing a major knee surgery, I was an avid runner. I live in Florida, and I loved to run right in the middle of the hot and humid days. I called it my microwave workout. But on one occasion, a night run worked better for my schedule. That night I was jogging along and thinking, *This feels great.* Then suddenly, out of the corner of my eye, I saw a shadow behind me. I freaked out and started sprinting. After a short while, I turned, looked again, and realized it was my own shadow. I felt relieved . . . and stupid.

Assuming that I was in danger after spotting this unexpected shadow was a natural human response. Sprinting might have kept me safe in a dangerous situation.

The assumption wasn't bad. My brain initiated the survival instinct of flight. However, to challenge my assumption and do what was optimal, I needed to move beyond my normal survival instinct and look again.

When we suspend and challenge our assumptions, we don't do away with them. We identify or clarify them so we can then verify or modify them. Suspending our natural assumptions, biases, and prejudices always leads to a win-win situation and provides us with more conviction about our decisions and more confidence in our execution.

When we challenge and then modify our assumptions, we may be saved from loss, embarrassment, or superficial fixes that backfire (and from needlessly sprinting in the dark).

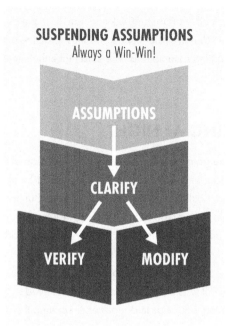

SUSPENDING ASSUMPTIONS
Always a Win-Win!

ASSUMPTIONS

CLARIFY

VERIFY   MODIFY

SNAPSHOTS AT WORK

Suppose your work colleague takes a snapshot of the sales team eating cake and drinking champagne before lunch. He comes to you, shares his snapshot, and says, "Can you believe those salespeople? They are always taking breaks and socializing during work hours. And they get rewarded for this behavior with big commissions."

You nod and say, "Yeah, that's life on the sales team."

Even if this assumption is accurate some of the time, it might not be true in this situation. You're applying the snapshot to the sales team's culture and reinforcing your colleague's bias.

Consider this alternate response.

"Well, they do seem to be throwing a party this morning. I wonder why?"

When your colleague asks around, he learns the sales team was celebrating the close of a big sale that put the company over its revenue target for the year. Several people on the team had collaborated to close the deal with the new client. The champagne and cake were for toasting the accomplishment and sharing the recognition.

The snapshot incriminated them; the movie vindicated them.

In healthy relationships and cultures, people assume good intentions until they look again and catch the movie that contradicts those good intentions.

OPTIMAL COMMUNICATION

Optimal communication is a highly effective leadership skill set that helps to create and reinforce a high-performance culture of respect. The aim is to use communication to gather correct and complete information so you can make the best decisions, improve relationships, and achieve optimal results. This requires two interrelated skills: suspending assumptions and optimal listening to capture both the content and the emotion.

Skills for suspending assumptions include observing, asking, and listening. You can't suspend assumptions without listening. And you can't listen optimally without suspending assumptions.

> You can't suspend assumptions without listening. And you can't listen optimally without suspending assumptions.

OPTIMAL LISTENING

Optimal listening is the ultimate way of showing respect to another person. It's the best way to look again. And if we're showing respect, we are making the other person realize we are suspending our assumptions and seeking to understand what they're saying. Listening builds a bridge to trust. Even when we are in the middle of an argument, if we are really listening, we are gaining influence and building trust in the relationship. And when leading change or dealing with diversity and polarization, remember: *They won't see what you see until you see what they see.* This requires you to take the initiative and model the behavior you desire from others.

If you want to persuade someone of something, seek to understand them first. Speak their language, allow them to speak their language, break down walls, and build a trusting relationship. When you are truly listening, you are suspending assumptions. You're listening to understand instead of to respond. Through listening, respect leads to trust and influence.

The more you listen, the more successful you will be in all areas of life, especially in relationships. The best salespeople are the best listeners. The best service people are the best listeners. The best leaders are the best listeners.

Whatever you are doing, whatever your function in life and at work, the more you practice optimal listening, the more successful you will be!

> The more you listen, the more successful you will be in all areas of life, especially in relationships.

FIVE LEVELS OF OPTIMAL LISTENING

Optimal listening has five levels. Each begins with "re-" because "re-" is associated with looking again.

Level 1: Reassure—Use short words or phrases to show you are listening.

Reassuring demonstrates your receptivity as you encourage the person to continue. This encouragement comes naturally when you are truly engaged in what the person is saying. Use words like: *Oh, wow. Really? Tell me more . . .*

When you reassure, the other person feels respected. This seems like a simple tactic, but it can result in seismic relationship shifts. One day after a session, a participant pulled me aside and confided, "I tried this reassure thing with my wife last night. She looked at me and said, 'There's something different about you today. I don't know what it is, but I like it!'"

Level 2: Repeat—Use a keyword from the other person that signals your understanding. When a direct report walks into your office and wants to talk, you probably have other things on your mind. To switch gears and listen better, take a word or two from what they said and simply repeat it back to them. This gets your brain into listening mode. It's like training wheels. This demonstrates respect and shows you are engaged. Of course, you don't want to overuse the repeat step and give the unintended perception that you're not listening to them. Try to avoid causing the response, "Yeah, that's what I just said!"

Level 3: Rephrase—Paraphrase in your own words what you heard the other person say. In John Powell's excellent book *Why Am I Afraid to Tell You Who I Am?* he writes: "I can never tell you what you said, but only what I heard. I will have to rephrase what you said, check it out with you to make sure what left your mind and heart arrived in my mind and heart without distortion."

Rephrasing clarifies the full picture of what the other person has in mind. If I tell you what I heard, you can tell me whether or not you meant what I heard. If not, you can clarify what you meant. This works wonders when your motive is to understand but not when you are trying to manipulate. When practiced with the right motive, rephrasing clarifies meaning and prevents misunderstandings.

Level 4: Reflect—Reflect content or feelings beneath the content that you hear in the message. In his book *People Skills*, Robert Bolton notes that reflection is "when the listener restates the feelings and/or content of what the speaker has communicated and does so in a way that demonstrates understanding and acceptance."

Reflection is important because we often skip over feelings. When you reflect back to the person any implied content or feelings, you take the conversation deeper. Once you understand how the person feels, you can often get to what they need.

Level 5: Review—When a person shares both content and emotion, you need to review the main points to confirm you captured the essence correctly. Listening at this level results in a remarkable depth of understanding and facilitates effective dialogue. If you do an effective review, you're likely saying it better or more succinctly than they are saying it.

> Reflection is important because
> we often skip over feelings.

LISTENING FOR IDEAS
AND INNOVATION

Now, suppose that while someone is talking, you get a good idea. If you quickly jot down what you heard the person say *and* your idea, you can maintain focus on listening. If you don't note your idea, you'll likely forget it or focus on remembering it and cease listening. It's often wise to tell the person that you're taking notes so they won't perceive this good intention as disrespect or distraction. This process works well in team meetings when we are searching for options and ideas. The point is to do both—to listen and capture good ideas—and still show respect.

This simple practice is powerful because it helps you suspend assumptions, see the movie, show respect, and get new ideas.

I find people rarely get the full meaning when they argue and advocate their positions, which often happens in team settings. If you employ the *review* level of listening properly, you can

REMEMBER TO USE THE
OPTIMAL LISTENING TOOL FOR NOTES

WHAT I HEAR:　　　　WHAT I THINK:

balance advocacy and inquiry. What comes naturally is to start out advocating—giving your opinion or defense. By contrast, what we do in review is see the movie and suspend assumptions before we proceed to a conclusion.

Optimal listening will win the day. Listening to one another's unique needs shows respect, builds trust, strengthens commitment, and expands influence.

LEADING CHANGE BY LISTENING

Often the problem with leading change isn't the plan or project—it's the heart and mind. You don't need people to conform to your vision. You need them to transform and adopt the vision. It isn't enough for people to agree. They must believe.

> Often the problem with leading change
> isn't the plan or the project—
> it's the heart and mind.

So how might we get them to believe? First, we acknowledge that everyone has a different reason for not believing. We start with respect by suspending our assumptions about what they think and believe. We listen. We gather observations. We exchange our snapshots for the whole movie.

Only then can we begin to value the differences that provide unique perspectives and valuable experience to our change initiatives.

Those who implement should have input.

VALUE DIFFERENCES

RESPECT > TRUST > INFLUENCE

SUSPEND ASSUMPTIONS   CULTIVATE OPENNESS   HONOR BOUNDARIES
VALUE DIFFERENCES   EXPAND DIALOGUE   CREATE LEADERS

By "differences" I mean the qualities that make each individual person unique. They may be physical, spiritual, philosophical, overt, or covert. They may involve race or class or age or background. It may mean what the marketing team brings to the table as opposed to what the finance people have to say. Valuing differences means intentionally seeking out differences of opinion, experience, or knowledge because all may contribute to a better result.

Valuing differences is foundational when leading change because it helps people believe. When you value differences, you create optimal input, participation, engagement, ownership, and accountability. When leaders ignore or fail to acknowledge differences, employees don't feel seen, and their unique contributions can be overlooked. A guiding principle for valuing differences is a key to respect: *those who implement should have input.*

Leaders who value differences also value diversity. They see differences as potential strengths. They understand how diverse beliefs, backgrounds, and experiences add value.

Let's be clear: valuing differences is not the same as accepting or tolerating differences to go along and get along. Valuing differences is the mindset and behavior that takes respect to the next level. Valuing differences also gets us closer to trust. When people feel valued and appreciated and like they truly belong, they're more likely to develop trust. And respect and trust are foundational to leading change.

> When people feel valued and appreciated
> and like they truly belong,
> they're more likely to develop trust.

MY FRIEND CARLOS

Early in my consulting career, I worked as a part-time leadership coach for my friend Carlos. He ran a counseling center in Charlotte, North Carolina. In addition to being a close friend, Carlos was an excellent counselor and highly competent business owner. Over the years he saved countless marriages and healed many families.

My job was to run small-group sessions for clients (mostly men) coming out of one-on-one counseling to help them improve their communication and relationship skills. Carlos also referred people to me for leadership coaching. Working with Carlos enabled me to create new content and integrate leadership concepts into my session designs.

Carlos's parents were from Ecuador, but he grew up in North Carolina in the 1980s. To say that there weren't many other Ecuadorians in his school or neighborhood is an understatement. And even though I inherited some Cherokee and Sicilian blood from my mother, I am as white as a bleached towel. I have never experienced racism.

One day I was having lunch with Carlos when he shared some stories of the painful prejudice he encountered while growing up. With honesty and the best of intentions, I quietly mustered what I thought was a kind response: "I never even think of you as Latino, Carlos. I never even consider it. To me, you're just my awesome friend."

Thinking that I'd get a positive response to my candor, I was shocked when Carlos paused, looked up, and with exasperated eyes replied, "That's the problem!"

I felt like a boulder had just landed on my head.

"What do you mean?" I asked.

"Don't you get what I've been telling you? I don't want to be seen simply as someone who's like everybody else. I want to be appreciated *because* I am Latino, *because* I was raised by immigrant parents. My ethnicity, my background, and my experiences make me unique. You can't just ignore my heritage and think you really know me or appreciate me. These are part of who I am. I want to be valued *because* of my Ecuadorian roots, not *despite* them."

My mouth gaped open, and I froze in silence for what seemed like several uncomfortable minutes. I then clumsily explained that my intent was to be colorblind, caring, and empathetic. But the longer I stammered, the deeper I dug myself into a hole under that boulder.

Then the "aha" hit me. I had no clue. In fact, I had no clue that I had no clue. Carlos, of course, was 100 percent spot-on. In a few miserable, yet magical minutes, I learned what valuing differences really meant from a friend who was close enough, kind enough, and brave enough to tell me the hard truth. He brought awareness to my boneheaded bias and challenged my noble intentions. I understood for the first time the impact of my words and actions. I got how failing to acknowledge and truly understand how someone is different has a negative impact.

VALUING DIFFERENCES AND DIVERSITY

When you value the differences among your team members, you build trust and gain influence. And when you're leading change, valuing differences is the best way to get uncommitted or polarized people to believe in the change initiative. Valuing differences broadens the scope of everything you do. It adds perspective and encourages innovative thinking. When stepping into new territory, every team and organization needs a broad platform of perspectives, skills, and experiences as a foundation.

The more you value differences, the more you show respect.

My mentor, Bob Pettus, told me that 90 percent of problems could be best resolved by valuing differences. My many years as a transformational change consultant and coach have proven that statement to be 100 percent correct.

The ability to value differences in the right way is particularly important for leaders, enabling them to survive and thrive in a disruptive global economy. It is the only way to reduce polarization. Conversely, valuing differences with ulterior motives leads to the tyranny of misguided tolerance, which leads to further polarization. We need not lose the hearts and souls of people in exchange for political expediency. We will survive and thrive to the degree we avoid the tyranny of intolerant tolerance (tolerating differences only when it fits our agenda). When we value differences, we trigger respect and optimize culture, input, innovation, collaboration, systems, and processes in any context.

A NEW APPROACH TO DIVERSITY, EQUITY, AND INCLUSION

Over the last decade, many organizations have implemented diversity, equity, and inclusion (DE&I) programs. While some have yielded improved cultures that truly value differences, many others have made little or no impact. And a few, forced upon employees for legal or public image reasons, have created more harm than good. Even when the intentions are noble, a poorly designed DE&I program can cause polarization. I've heard participants complain, "All I learned was how different we all are," or "Now I'm afraid to say anything because I might offend somebody." These attitudes reflect the complicated nature of this emotionally charged issue.

In an eye-opening *Harvard Business Review* article titled "Why Diversity Initiatives Fail—And What Works Better," Frank Dobbin and Alexandra Kalev show how making a diversity transformation part of a larger change initiative has better results than most non-systemic diversity programs. They write: "In analyzing three decades' worth of data from more than 800 U.S. firms and interviewing hundreds of line managers and executives at length, we've seen that companies get better results when they ease up on the control tactics. It's more effective to engage managers in solving the problem, increase their on-the-job contact with female and minority workers, and promote social accountability—the desire to look fair-minded. That's why interventions such as targeted college recruitment, mentoring programs, self-managed teams, and task forces have boosted diversity in businesses. Some of the most effective solutions aren't even designed with diversity in mind."

SEVEN CHARACTERISTICS OF A SUCCESSFUL DE&I PROCESS

In my experience, trying to make people participate in or conform to a DE&I program often backfires because it focuses on symptoms rather than on root issues. To be effective, a good DE&I initiative must transform the awareness, behavior, and culture of your teams. They must be processes, designed with seven characteristics:

1. **Broad**. Valuing differences must extend beyond race to all areas of teams, organizations, and society. When

combining personalities, perspectives, capabilities, and functions, countless differences come into play.

2. **Ethical and Business Minded**. The ethical case for valuing differences—*it's the right thing to do*—and the business case—*it's the profitable thing to do*—must blend.

3. **Value-Oriented**. It's not just about a passive request to get along. DE&I must be active and proactive, tied to business goals, productivity goals, or profitability goals.

4. **Culture-Focused**. Successful DE&I processes avoid specific emotionally charged incidents and instead focus on shared cultural values. They explore root issues that apply to all areas of the organization.

5. **Transformation-Focused.** They must be focused on transforming the system, the ultimate context for leading change. A training program won't do it. Most diversity initiatives are implemented by choosing diversity team task force members who are diverse, care deeply about the issues, and take their roles seriously. However, the team is not always chosen based on whether they are transformers first and foremost.

6. **Sustainable Process**. Successful DE&I processes are not just another flavor-of-the-month program. They involve leadership, teams, systems, and culture. They include programs for developing leadership capabilities such as interpersonal skills, communication, listening, dialogue, innovation, and skillful negotiation.

7. **Possibility Thinking**. They turn conflict into creativity, ideas into innovation, and dialogue into development through valuing differences.

START WITH IE&D?

Do we have it backward? Perhaps we should start with the "I"? An *inclusive leadership* model creates an open and safe environment for confronting difficult issues regardless of functional, operational, or cultural differences. This results in both diversity and equity. Valuing differences lays the groundwork for inclusion. It plays a vital role in successful teams, especially in multinational organizations.

Accepting differences is the ethical thing to do. Valuing differences is both the ethical and the profitable thing to do. The "I" is about optimizing relationships and results.

> Valuing differences is both the ethical and the profitable thing to do. It's about optimizing relationships and results.

A BETTER PATH

Kevin A. Henry, chief human resources officer at a bottler of the largest soft drink company in the world, was a passionate DE&I advocate. He had noticed that many DE&I programs had good messages but often failed to create lasting change.

Instead of pulling people together and cultivating openness and dialogue, these well-intentioned programs tended to push people apart. They seemed to underemphasize the messages of unity, common values, shared vision, and the universal longing for belonging, dignity, and respect.

As an experienced C-suite executive who was also African American, Kevin knew there had to be a better path—a way to inspire authentic and sustainable transformational change. So Kevin and the senior leadership team set a guiding principle that informed their strategy: because valuing differences is both ethical and profitable, they would build it into their culture, systems, and structure. If they could focus on valuing differences—operations, marketing, accounting, sales, and HR, male and female, black and white, north and south—all these would become assets, valuable points of view. They wouldn't focus on symptoms. They would encourage the mindsets and behavior norms that value differences of circumstances, backgrounds, and beliefs. And if an employee couldn't align with the guiding principle, they would invite the employee to find a company that thought like they did.

Kevin and I collaborated to create a valuing differences initiative that evolved into a valuing differences equation. Since its implementation almost twenty years ago, the company has become the leading beverage manufacturer and distributor in its national system in terms of innovation and profits. Its growth and profit strategy has included the acquisition of other beverage companies and the merging of disparate cultures into one, guided by their valuing differences principle. This strategy helped them transform their system and culture, stay true to their vision through inclusive leadership, and increase their profits through successful acquisitions.

Valuing differences needs to be a foundational part of the culture because it is the best way to create or fix processes and systems. You can't change the system with snapshots. Valuing differences is the optimal way to get the full movie, tear down functional silos, and encourage cross-functional collaboration. It's not just a feel-good activity. It's about making the business run better. For optimal results, the valuing differences equation becomes both the system and what fixes and sustains the system.

VALUING DIFFERENCES EQUATION

Valuing differences is not only a precursor to personal trust but also the best way to create an organization-wide culture of trust. That is why I designed the valuing differences equation, with Kevin Henry's input, as the foundation of my *Start with Respect* model.

VALUING DIFFERENCES EQUATION

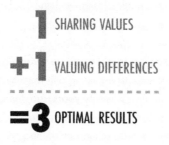

1 SHARING VALUES

+1 VALUING DIFFERENCES

=3 OPTIMAL RESULTS

I know from hard-won experience, case studies, and coaching leaders worldwide that valuing differences is the unsung hero for building change capability and leading change because it always enhances:

- Respect, trust, influence
- Input
- Participation
- Ownership
- Accountability
- Engagement
- Information flow

- Communication processes
- Problem-solving
- Decision-making
- Dialogue
- Innovation
- Collaboration
- Systems thinking

- Process improvement
- Feedback
- Belief, buy-in, and commitment
- Culture and morale
- Overcoming resistance
- Reducing polarization
- Sales
- Customer service
- Coaching and developing leaders

This is the beauty of valuing differences. By focusing on one thing, you can bring optimal results to multiple initiatives.

Valuing differences requires us to suspend assumptions and practice optimal listening, which leads to appreciation and respect. Only after we have mastered this leap can we turn our attention to developing a culture of trust.

Interested in diving deeper into Respect?
Download more resources and tools at
startwithrespect.com.

If I say the truth, will what I say be used against me?

DEFINING TRUST

RESPECT ❯ **TRUST** ❯ INFLUENCE

Trust is the glue to every good relationship, professional or personal. And the tricky thing is that everyone's take on trust is different. Some people start with "I won't trust until you earn my trust." Others begin with "I'll trust until you give me a reason not to trust." So how do you build trust when the meaning is so nebulous?

This is where it is optimal to start with respect to get to trust. If you show respect by suspending assumptions and valuing differences, you can increase the level of trust with any person or situation.

> If you show respect by suspending assumptions and valuing differences, you can increase the level of trust with any person or situation.

TRUST AND ASSUMPTIONS

Like respect, trust is connected to our assumptions. For example, I trust a chair because I assume it will hold me up. I trust cooks at a restaurant because I assume they won't poison me. I trust pilots of airplanes because I assume they know how to fly a plane, and I trust the plane because I assume it has been maintained properly.

Now, if I've broken chairs in the past, know someone who has been poisoned in a restaurant, or a read about a recent plane crash in the news, I may decide to change my assumptions. My trust becomes tenuous.

Assumptions are based on past experiences, and everyone has different experiences that affect their trust threshold. When it comes to leading change, our level of trust often has to do with what we know about the past successes and failures of our leaders.

Most people who don't trust have good reasons, so they often resist change. Therefore, when leading change, we need to increase the level of trust with multiple people in multiple situations. Showing respect can even the ground and pave the path to greater trust.

NATURE AND NURTURE OF TRUST

We all know how important trust is, but we rarely stop to think about the nature of trust. What are some of its features?

Trust is a perception. Many times, trust is based on perceptions, not on objective reality. That's why we need to communicate in such a way that perceptions match our intentions. Showing respect by suspending assumptions and valuing differences will help us better understand the trust perceptions of other people.

Trust is dynamic. You may have high trust this morning and low trust this afternoon. The trust level is constantly changing, depending on the level of trustworthy behavior, perceived or real.

Trust is risky. Trust always involves risk. When we show respect, we mitigate the trust risk and make transformation easier to navigate.

> When we show respect,
> we mitigate the trust risk and make
> transformation easier to navigate.

Trust is fragile. You can build a trusting relationship with someone for twenty years, but it can be gone in an instant—and you may never get it back! Sometimes you can win it back, but you are always at the mercy of the other person.

Trust is fragile not only in our personal lives but also among our teams, in our organizations, and with our customers. If our organization has failed to lead change in the past, we may find it difficult to convince participants to trust the present change initiative.

Trust shows up as an emotion. Like respect, trust shows up as an emotion. We can't keep emotions out of the workplace—not if we want to build trust. Obviously, we want to keep emotions appropriate and professional at work, but we can't shut them down and deny the role emotions play in cultivating trust. Trust has an emotional component whether we acknowledge it or not.

TRUST ENVIRONMENT

Many organizations fail to cultivate the sort of open and transparent environment that is key to nurturing trust. A trust-friendly environment can be ruined by a single statement, policy, hire, promotion, response, lack of response, or untimely response. Trust must be cultivated like a vulnerable garden.

In his excellent book *Reaching Out*, David W. Johnson writes: "In order to create trust, you must learn to create a climate of trust that reduces your own and the other person's fears of betrayal and rejection and promotes the hopes of acceptance, support, and confirmation." One untrustworthy person on a team will lower the combined level of trust on the whole team.

WISDOM OF SOLOMON

Just as one major, obvious action can change the trust dynamic quickly, smaller and more subtle actions can destroy trust over time. The wise Solomon once wrote a poem to his lover that said, "Catch the small foxes for they spoil the vine." What did he mean? The big foxes are what we usually look for because they can reach the grapes. Small foxes can't reach the grapes, but they can chew the vine. When the small foxes chew the vine, they destroy the whole system. Small, intangible things—like making assumptions, listening poorly, or not valuing differences—can destroy trust in relationships. Little by little, we feel disrespected or rejected. Suddenly we can't work together anymore. And if we can't work together, the situation incrementally gets worse and worse. Now we start working around each other. We ruin the system. We need to focus on the small foxes before they do big damage.

Often, it's not the plans or the execution of plans that bring a leader or organization down, making them a victim of change and disruption. It's the atmosphere, the environment, the culture. The system gets its breath from the atmosphere. It gets its life from the atmosphere. It dies when the atmosphere becomes toxic. An environment of disrespect poisons trust. A respect environment allows us to breathe trust.

An environment of disrespect poisons trust.
A respect environment allows us
to breathe trust.

Trust requires the willingness to be open to and open with other people!

Many other concepts relate to trust, such as integrity, candor, authenticity, consistency, congruency, expertise, empathy, and trustworthiness. In the chapters that follow, I will focus on two elements that we can apply to reduce resistance and polarization when leading transformational change: *cultivate openness* and *expand dialogue*. These two critical elements encourage deeper trust and determine the quality of input, innovation, and tangible results.

The first step is to *cultivate openness*. Openness must be cultivated like a garden. Untrustworthy and misaligned actions must be pulled like weeds. Credibility, consistency, candor, integrity, and congruence must always rain down. And watchful eyes must protect the crop from disease or scavengers.

The level of openness always affects results: *openness determines outcomes*.

The second step is to *expand dialogue*. Without dialogue there will be limited input, information, innovation, conversation, understanding, and results. In a context of leading change, dialogue facilitates the flow of relevant information so that you can make the best decisions, solve root problems, overcome resistance, create innovative strategies, increase agility, improve communication, and create options. The level of openness will always determine the level of dialogue, which differs from discussion. Paradoxically, the best way to find solutions is not to look for solutions but to create options. Openness enables us to expand our dialogue and create better options. Again, *the best way to find a solution is to create options*.

Openness determines outcomes.

CULTIVATE OPENNESS

RESPECT ❯	TRUST ❯	INFLUENCE
SUSPEND ASSUMPTIONS	CULTIVATE OPENNESS	HONOR BOUNDARIES
VALUE DIFFERENCES	EXPAND DIALOGUE	CREATE LEADERS

Once we start suspending our assumptions and valuing the differences of the people we live and work with, we can begin to cultivate a culture of openness. When people feel respected, when they trust that telling the truth or delivering bad news won't lead to unfair retribution, they are much more likely to be open and vulnerable.

To create a culture of openness, grounded in trust, leaders must consistently solicit and accept truthful, fact-based information—the good, the bad, and the ugly! People need to be assured that sharing bad news, disappointing results, complicated feelings, or unpopular perspectives won't be held against them. When they feel supported *after* they share information, they are more likely to share more. It's the snowball effect. When information is accepted and acted upon, and when truth-tellers are supported, they are more willing to share more information.

Cultivating a culture of openness is like forming a reinforcing loop.

TRUTH TELLING

It was one of those high-stakes, do-or-die meetings.

The top executives were discussing recent industry disruptions, trying to figure out the company's next move. They asked a few key department representatives to join the meeting and address hypothetical situations to determine the company's exposure and risk.

Dan was representing the risk management department. Keenly aware of the meeting's significance, he diligently prepared. When the meeting time arrived, his heart was pounding. He took a deep breath, wiped his sweaty palms on his pants, and walked into the conference room. The pressure was on.

The executives hurled questions at Dan. He came back with solid, and occasionally brilliant, responses.

Then one senior executive threw out a question that Dan hadn't researched. For a split second, he contemplated skirting the question. Since this was his area of expertise, the other execs would probably not know the difference.

As he glanced across the room, Dan realized that the right thing to do in this critical moment was to tell the complete truth; otherwise, he would be letting down these executives, his department, his company, and ultimately himself. This wasn't a time to protect his image. Telling the truth was more important.

Dan took a deep breath and quietly spoke. "I'll be honest. I don't know. I didn't consider that scenario. I just don't know." His gaze dropped to the floor.

The senior executive, focused on the substantial business vulnerability related to the question, responded with an icy demand. "That information is critical. We need you to know and to let us know, ASAP."

Red-faced, Dan swiftly left the room.

Bob, the chief HR officer, sprang out of his chair, swung the door open, and sprinted down the hall after Dan. The executives left in the room glanced at each other, perplexed by Bob's urgent exit.

Bob caught up with Dan just as he was pressing the elevator button. "Wait a minute, Dan. I need to tell you something."

Dan looked up, nervous for what was coming next. Bob gently placed his hand on Dan's shoulder. "You did an important thing just now, Dan. It took a lot of guts to admit that you didn't know the answer. I've been trying to promote that kind of honesty and integrity in our culture. Thank you for modeling it back there."

Shocked by the turn of event, Dan stammered, "Thank you, sir."

"No, thank you. Hurry back when you find the answer. We're counting on you."

LESSONS IN THE STORY

Some subtle lessons embedded in this story are worth exploring.

- Would Dan have been brave enough to admit that he didn't have the answer if, at some level, a culture of trust hadn't been building in the company?
- How much did it cost Bob to leave the meeting and catch up with Dan at the elevator? What difference did it make to Dan?
- How could this story be used to reinforce the kind of culture that Bob is trying to build at the company?
- How could Dan's experience influence how bad news is shared in the future?

CREATING A CULTURE OF OPENNESS

A culture of openness flows in a circular, self-sustaining pattern. This open-environment concept was adapted from David W. Johnson's book *Reaching Out*.

When people can express themselves without the fear of judgment, they feel accepted and respected. That's why the ultimate trust test is: *If I express myself, will what I say be used against me?* A negative answer to that question leads to a trusting environment where more people are willing to speak up and tell the truth, even when it's a hard truth. Correct and complete information will lead to more optimal decision-making and problem-solving. When people feel supported or perhaps even celebrated for their openness, more trust is built and reinforced.

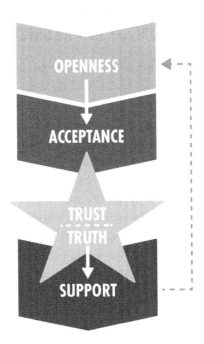

When leaders cultivate a culture of openness, the quality of dialogue among individuals and teams improves. Instead of becoming defensive or stubbornly advocating for a position, people set aside their ego, listen, look beyond obvious either-or solutions, and innovate.

> When people can express themselves
> without the fear of judgment, they feel
> accepted and respected.

FEAR, POLITICS, AND SUPPRESSION OF EXPRESSION

In his article "Suppression of Expression: An Unintended Consequence of Top-Down Leadership," my friend and mentor Ken Shelton writes:

> "When good men and women are made to sit down or put down and told to shut up and denied formal recognition in the system of their good nature and good works, others take notice and either voluntarily or involuntarily suppress their expression. They become afraid to speak up and out and especially afraid to put their ideas in writing and distribute or publish them. They confine their expressions to safe locations, occasions, and audiences, and even then, they are very careful not to offend. In most cases, this self-censorship is voluntary, not mandatory, but it is just as effective."

When openness is not rewarded, when it is frowned upon or discouraged either openly or subtly, a culture of fear takes hold. Negative news is suppressed for fear of political repercussions.

CULTURE BEFORE STRATEGY

By now, I hope you realize that the optimal culture of a high-performing organization is one anchored in trust and designed to actively encourage openness. Effective leaders understand that they must get their culture right before turning their attention to strategy and planning. As Peter Drucker famously said, "Culture eats strategy for breakfast." The degree to which people are comfortable being open and honest will determine how they define reality, how they view the organization and their role, how they relate and interact with others, and how often they engage in constructive dialogue. Openness generates the groundwork for an effective strategy and facilitates implementation of the strategic plan. In short, *openness determines outcomes.*

> Effective leaders understand that they must get their culture right before turning their attention to strategy and planning.

GRAPES AND INTEGRITY

The Hebrew word for integrity is *tom,* from the root word *tamam,* which means integrity and much more. It is also the word for perfection, completion, and wholeness. In ancient times, clean drinking water was often hard to come by, so wine and grape juice were common substitutes at meals. The ideal time for harvesting the grapes that produced the best wine and juice was at their ripest point—when they were complete, whole. This was the moment the grape's *integrity* was at its peak.

This provides a memorable analogy for cultivating an open culture where integrity can flourish. Leaders must nurture and cultivate it, especially when the vines are young and tender.

THE LAST WORDS ON OPENNESS— MUTUAL RESPECT

A culture of openness requires people to act consistently with mutual respect. Having an open culture doesn't provide a license to belittle others or to violate their personal boundaries. Instead, it keeps the balance between respecting ourselves and the truth we are obligated to share and respecting our colleagues and their thoughts and opinions. Yes, it can be a delicate balance at times. You might think of it this way: *say what you mean without being mean*.

When we are leading change, we need to get all the relevant information, real or perceived, from different perspectives. Leaders must create a culture of openness because openness determines outcomes, especially when leading change.

The best way to find a solution is not to look for a solution but to create options.

EXPAND DIALOGUE

RESPECT ❯ TRUST ❯ INFLUENCE

SUSPEND ASSUMPTIONS   CULTIVATE OPENNESS   HONOR BOUNDARIES
VALUE DIFFERENCES   EXPAND DIALOGUE   CREATE LEADERS

Since today's workplace is teeming with complex problems, leaders may feel stuck when addressing complicated challenges. Expanding dialogue provides more options and better outcomes.

In his book *Dialogue: The Art of Thinking Out Loud Together*, William Issacs, a pioneer in innovative dialogue, summarizes the etymology and meaning of dialogue: "The roots of the word *dialogue* come from the Greek words *dia* and *logos*. *Dia* means 'through'; *logos* translates to 'word' or 'meaning'. In essence, a dialogue is a flow of meaning. In the ancient meaning, *logos* meant 'to gather together', and suggested an intimate awareness of the relationships among things in the natural world. *Dialogue* is a conversation in which people think together in relationship. *Thinking together* implies that you no longer take your own position as final. You relax your grip on certainty and listen to the possibilities that result simply from being in a relationship with others—possibilities that might not otherwise have occurred."

So how can leaders expand dialogue and use it to solve problems and make decisions?

The degree to which leaders cultivate an open culture determines the level of dialogue in the culture. Dialogue can only happen when people trust that their ideas and views can be expressed without fear of judgment.

Dialogue is a two-way (or multiple-way, when it involves more than two people), open-ended sharing of ideas. During dialogue, the conversation flows from one person to another, igniting and integrating new thought patterns. It values diverse viewpoints. Participants are able to suspend their assumptions and their distinct perspectives. The intention of dialogue is not to reach an immediate decision but to create space for an open exchange of ideas and options. Alternatively, discussion involves debate. It pulls together opinions and facts and immediately converges them into a collective viewpoint or decision.

CONDITIONS FOR A CULTURE OF DIALOGUE

There are six conditions that help leaders facilitate dialogue:

- Safety to think out loud
- Freedom to speak without interruptions or criticism
- Valuing differences
- Freedom to think laterally
- Respect for the contributions of others
- Careful and accurate listening

Dialogue that results in innovative breakthroughs starts when team members feel completely comfortable sharing their ideas. It is nurtured when colleagues refrain from interrupting, when they are open to ideas and respectfully consider them as alternatives to their own thinking about the problem. It takes root when leaders give credit and praise for diverse contributions and possibility thinking.

> Dialogue that results in innovative breakthroughs starts when team members feel completely comfortable sharing their ideas.

LISTENING AND DIALOGUE

In dialogue, we utilize the five levels of optimal listening—Reassure, Repeat, Rephrase, Reflect, and Review. These tools assist both parties in suspending assumptions and listening with an open mind to capture facts, thoughts, feelings, needs, and wants.

LEON AND ALICIA

Leon and Alicia work for a snack manufacturer and distributor.

Leon is the general manager at a branch with a cult-like following. Over the years, Leon and his branch colleagues have concluded that corporate headquarters inhibits branch sales, does not support branch activities, and fails to understand what it takes to sell a product and service a client. As a result, Leon has refused to align with many corporate processes.

Alicia manages the corporate finance department. Her job requires her to advise branch managers on certain parameters related to pricing and discounts. While she is the ultimate decision-maker, she is also often the middle person, balancing the opinions of the brand team with the customer demands that flow from the branch managers. She has noticed that Leon often gives her incomplete or inaccurate data and impossibly short deadlines for her responses. He doesn't hesitate to go around her if she doesn't get back to him quickly enough or if he doesn't like her response. She is fairly certain that he doesn't understand or care about the impact of ignoring corporate processes.

Tensions became so severe between these two managers that the company hired me to mediate a session with them. I started by explaining my ground rules.

"Leon and Alicia, both of you will have the chance to share your perspective on the issues that have been brewing between you and your teams. Alicia will go first by stating what she sees as the problem that has developed between the two of you. Leon, please take detailed notes on what you hear Alicia say.

This will help you suspend your assumptions. Alicia, please go slowly so Leon can take good notes.

"When Alicia is done, Leon, I'd like you to rephrase what you heard her say. She will then fill in any gaps you didn't articulate or will clarify what she meant to say. Please refrain from refuting, defending, or responding to what she says. Please don't be offended if I interrupt you if you begin to defend your position or refute what Alicia is saying. I will ask her to follow the same guidelines when it's your turn, so you will have ample opportunity to share your perspective."

As each person spoke, the other could barely stop themselves from jumping in to defend their position. This was when I reminded them to suspend their assumptions and work through the levels of optimal listening. It is vital to get to the *reflect* level of listening because that is when feelings surface, often revealing the crux of the problem.

As Alicia reflected, she shared, "I don't feel like Leon and his branch members respect me and my department. They don't seem to value what I do."

When it was Leon's time to share, he said the same thing: "I don't feel like Alicia or corporate respects me and what we do at the branch."

I find that feeling disrespected is almost always at the root of the issue. Creating a safe space for open dialogue and utilizing the five levels of optimal listening helped Leon and Alicia see their intent versus their impact. Leon had the noble intent to help the customer. He was upset because Alicia didn't respond to him fast enough, especially when he was in front of a customer in a sales or service situation. Alicia also had good intent. She wanted to use the right process and provide accurate information. Sometimes she was forced to wait to get accurate information so she could give Leon and his team the best possible answer.

> Feeling disrespected is almost always
> at the root of the issue.

Once Leon and Alicia both felt heard and respected, we continued with a dialogue to create options. I asked them what they needed from each other to feel respected and get the best results. Among other things, Leon stated: "I need an answer. I need to know what to tell the customer in front of me."

And Alicia said, "I need you to trust that I am working on an answer and that I'll get back to you as soon as possible."

Clarity began to surface. What Leon really needed was a *response*, not an answer. Alicia assumed he needed an answer. Leon reinforced this assumption when he asked for what he thought he needed instead of clearly defining what he really needed.

FROM ADVERSARIES TO COLLEAGUES

Once Leon and Alicia expressed that they felt disrespected, their vulnerability established a shared understanding that fostered a surprising degree of empathy. They let down their guard and began talking to each other as caring colleagues instead of adversaries. They created options that led to a solution that felt satisfactory to both parties.

In his classic book *The Fifth Discipline*, Peter Senge notes: "Dialogue can occur only when a group of people see each other as colleagues in mutual quest for deeper insight and clarity. The conscious act of thinking of one another as colleagues contributes toward interacting as colleagues." Seeing each other as colleagues and friends sets a positive tone and offsets the vulnerability that dialogue brings. People feel that they are building deeper understanding.

SURVEY AND MAP THE TERRITORY

When leaders guide their teams toward expanding their dialogue to create innovative options, their first steps are to survey and map the territory. It's important that they identify various stakeholders' positions, clarify the meaning and consequences of change, look for possibilities and opportunities, decide the direction—where to go and where not to go—and develop a vision for the new territory.

Their teams may feel stuck, trapped, or out of options for several reasons: outdated and ineffective ways of doing things, old attitudes and habitual behaviors, outdated processes and procedures, ineffective technology, resistance to learning new skills, silos and hierarchical structures, old assumptions about customers, outdated management and leadership styles, poor communication, ineffective recruiting and hiring, lagging behind industry trends and stalled innovation, reacting instead of anticipating change, playing politics, or ignoring demographic shifts. Dialogue is the key to getting past all these hurdles.

When leaders survey the territory, they step out of their office, ask questions, think outside the box, and refuse to accept the status quo. It is a proactive, positive, and structured activity with a specific purpose: to identify clearly where you are in the process before starting the change initiative.

> It's important to develop a vision
> for the new territory.

4-D FACILITATION—DIALOGUE FOR OPTIONS

I created 4-D facilitation as a dialogue model that utilizes suspending assumptions and valuing differences as leverage points for showing respect and building mutual trust. It's a versatile tool that can be used for conversation, facilitation, innovation, negotiation, or mediation.

Here is how it works.

The 4 D's are **D**ialogue, **D**iscuss, **D**ecide, and **D**o or Delegate: Dialogue focuses on creating options; Discuss focuses on determining possible solutions; Decide focuses on an agreed-upon resolution; and Do or Delegate focuses on execution.

When people are polarized, they tend to dig in their heels and advocate for their position rather than get curious and listen to others' points of view. In contrast, 4-D facilitation starts with respect and dialogue. It creates a positive pull in our efforts to transform teams and cultures. Embedded in the concept of dialogue are suspending assumptions, optimal listening, valuing differences, and an open environment. We *look again* to make sure we include all snapshots to get the full movie.

THE SOLUTION PARADOX

The strategy behind 4-D is what I call the solution paradox: *the best way to find a solution is not to look for a solution but to create options.*

While it's a natural tendency to focus on solutions, it is not optimal. For example, when we are faced with a complex problem or difficult decision, we find it natural to gather smart leaders in a conference room and focus on solving the problem or making a decision. With good intentions and a desire to be efficient, we jump to solve instead of first expanding our options. This path cuts short the dialogue process, often leaving out better options or possibilities.

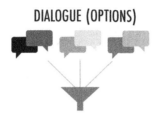

DIALOGUE (OPTIONS)

DISCUSS FOR SOLUTIONS

The goal of discussion is to find solutions from our options. *Discuss* has the same Latin root word as *percussion* and *concussion*, meaning to smash against. It can be called ping-pong conversation or billiard-ball conversation. It is meant to bring out views to test and challenge them.

When one person starts to dialogue and another person starts to discuss, the conversation moves to discussion by default. As a result, few people, especially in groups, spend much time in true dialogue. This limits options and possibilities. We default to a black-and-white world when we could be thriving in 3-D (or 4-D), high-resolution color!

When one person starts to dialogue and another person starts to discuss, the conversation moves to discussion by default.

Optimal team learning only takes place when there is a synergy between the two conversation styles of dialogue and discussion. Again, the key strategy is to be aware of when the group is in either dialogue or discussion.

THE GROAN ZONE

Dialogue represents diversity and divergent viewpoints; discussion represents the convergent, collective viewpoint. The result is diverse consensus. This graphic (adapted from Sam Kaner's *Facilitator's Guide to Participatory Decision-Making*) shows what happens in dialogue and discussion and why they are difficult to maintain. The problem arises when there is a divergence from a solution due to people with different perspectives bringing up multiple new ideas. The people who are solution focused rather than option focused begin to feel annoyed, distracted, or impatient. This is the groan zone, or what is sometimes called the turbulent zone.

Most teams are so focused on quickly finding a solution that they can't handle the groan zone.

Most teams are so focused on quickly finding a solution that they can't handle the groan zone. However, it is optimal to maintain dialogue long enough to create more options and possibilities in the turbulent zone before converging on solutions. This leads to better solutions and decisions. And when divergent inputs are accepted with respect via suspending assumptions and valuing differences, it will create better results and more engagement, participation, accountability, and ultimately trust.

As a facilitator, I place a name tent on the table with "dialogue" and "discuss" written on either side to inform participants when we are using each skill. After some practice, they no longer need the card. During conversations it helps to have a way of indicating what to do and when. For example, some people do this intuitively by declaring "I'm playing devil's advocate" when they choose to move from dialogue to discussion or debate.

Discussion often surfaces things we didn't consider during the initial dialogue. In these situations, leaders or facilitators can guide the group back to dialogue so they can create more or better options.

BEAUTY OF THE THIRD OPTION

When reaching the end of the discuss phase, I require groups to have at least three options to choose from before we move to the decide stage. Requiring a third option moves the group away from either-or scenarios and into a both-and scenario, which tends to be more creative and innovative. Once teams experience the beauty of the third option, they often further expand dialogue to seek fourth and fifth options.

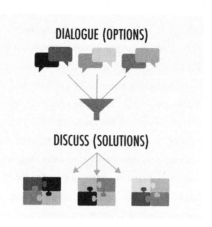

DIALOGUE (OPTIONS)

DISCUSS (SOLUTIONS)

If the leader or facilitator doesn't force a third option, especially when people are polarized, the either-or scenario tends to reinforce polarization, and the whole process can backfire.

> Requiring a third option moves the group away from either-or scenarios and into a both-and scenario, which tends to be more creative and innovative.

DECIDE FOR RESOLUTION

The goal of the decide stage is to create a resolution from our dialogue and discussion. The English word *decide* comes from the Latin *decidere*, meaning to murder or kill an alternative. This etymology acts as a suitable metaphor for our purposes. If we are going to execute one or more options after dialogue and discussion, we should first conduct a fair trial, which leads to a clear resolution and confidence to execute. It is easier to execute when we are committed to the decision after having a thorough and fair trial.

Using 4-D doesn't mean all decisions must be done by consensus. The leader is still responsible for making decisions. However, dialogue and discussion are the optimal platforms for building respect and trust, adding multiple perspectives, making the best decisions, and gaining more engagement for execution.

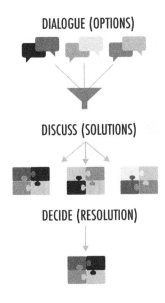

DIALOGUE (OPTIONS)

DISCUSS (SOLUTIONS)

DECIDE (RESOLUTION)

DO (OR DELEGATE) FOR EXECUTION

Once the team has decided, they can either do or delegate and follow up for accountability. Since we started with dialogue and discussion based on respect and trust, we will see more ownership and engagement for execution and accountability as an output of the process.

DIALOGUE (OPTIONS)

DISCUSS (SOLUTIONS)

DECIDE (RESOLUTION)

DO/DELEGATE (EXECUTION)

IS YOUR TEAM LEVERAGING THE POWER OF DIALOGUE?

Ask yourself and your team members:

- Are we thinking out loud, or are we keeping our thoughts to ourselves?
- Are we focused on possibilities and options rather than only solutions?
- Are we getting impractical or "crazy" ideas, or are we playing safe?
- Did the idea or partial idea from someone spawn a new idea from someone else?

Never forget, the best way to find a solution is not to look for a solution but to create options.

Interested in diving deeper into Trust?
Download more resources and tools at
startwithrespect.com.

Leadership is influence.

DEFINING INFLUENCE

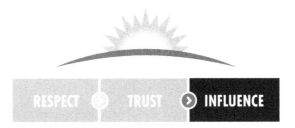

RESPECT | TRUST | INFLUENCE

What's the first thought that comes to mind when you hear the word *influence*? Many people think of social media influencers with thousands of followers. Some are worthy of the word; others, not so much. For some people, influence may have a negative connotation, such as "He's a bad influence on my child." But most of the time, we see influence as a positive reference to someone who has earned credibility from their character, conduct, capabilities, or power to persuade.

When I'm talking about influence in the context of leading change through RTI, I am speaking about influence born from trust and credibility in contrast to control through fear and intimidation. Leading change through influence is more about *pulling* people to transform than *pushing* people to conform or reform.

> Leading change through influence is more about *pulling* people to transform than *pushing* people to conform or reform.

Think about a time when you were pushed toward change. Perhaps your spouse, partner, or friend decided they wanted to go out to the movies on Friday instead of enjoying the usual popcorn and Netflix on the couch. You were pushed—rather than pulled—to go along with the change even though you were tired from a hectic week at work. How did you feel as you sat in the theater? What would a "pull" conversation have sounded like, and would it have made you feel different?

Influence differs from control or manipulation, just as intent differs from impact. For example, I may have good intent when I try to positively influence my team during a change initiative.

However, if the people I'm leading *feel* they are being manipulated, the impact becomes the opposite of my intent. If they perceive the change as coercive, they tend to push back. This creates a push-push dynamic and creates a spiral of resistance and polarization.

When something is pushed on you, when you don't have any input, when you don't agree with it or believe in it, when you haven't even thought about it, you suspect that someone is trying to manipulate you. This causes you to become angry, upset, pressured, stressed, discouraged, or frustrated.

HOW MATTERS

It's natural to push people to conform; it's optimal to pull people to transform. Some things may get done faster by pushing, but *how* you get there is as important as the destination because of its impact on sustainability.

> Some things may get done faster
> by pushing, but *how* you get there
> is as important as the destination because
> of its impact on sustainability.

For example, if you want to get to the airport in your SUV in twenty minutes (normally a thirty-minute trip), you will need to push to get that result. This will involve speeding, perhaps even banging the SUV against curbs and other cars, running stoplights, and harming others in the process.

Made it! Done. Minutes to spare. Results.

Sure, you made it. You can feel relieved about not getting caught running the light or sideswiping the car. You can feel clever for not hitting a biker or killing a dog. However, you did bang up your new ride, put others in danger, look like an idiot, and get a few heart-rate warnings from your digital watch.

And your reckless driving has a permanent impact. The more you repeat this short-sighted stupidity, the more it destroys your vehicle, stresses everyone, harms others, reduces your net results, and causes terror on the road. Worst of all, if you get away with it, you'll keep doing it because you got results, you got there fast, and you will likely be rewarded for it again!

In contrast, influence as an output of respect and trust creates sustainable change because it works through a pull dynamic that forms a leaders-of-leaders system and culture. In this case, the *how* becomes the secret to the sustainable *what*. You get to the airport, the SUV is intact, you avoid collateral damage, and others want to ride with you.

In the next section, we use *influence* as a synonym for *leadership*. Defining leadership as influence expands the scope beyond positional leadership to include personal leadership. Hence, anyone who influences is a leader whether they have a position or not. When viewing leadership through this lens, the question isn't *if* you're a leader but instead *what kind* of leader you are and *how* you're leading.

CREATING MORE LEADERS

When those who lack the title of leader start viewing themselves as leaders, they transcend paradigms and establish a foundation for a leaders-of-leaders culture. This paradigm changes the behavior of both non-positional leaders and positional leaders.

Holding everyone accountable for showing respect leads to more trust and influence and embeds the paradigm into the team or organization.

If leadership at its core is influence, we can speak of creators of leaders as *influencers of influencers*. Since the output of RTI is influence, RTI becomes the optimal way to nurture a broad-based leadership culture. The more influencers of influencers we develop, the less likely we are to get stuck in reactor mode, and the greater our change capability.

Understanding what Stephen R. Covey refers to as "circles of influence" is key to establishing a leaders-of-leaders culture. Circles of influence represent the individuals and groups that fall within the influence range of a person. We can use the potential power of the ripple effect of circles of influence to lead change effectively. Each circle of influence creates reinforcing loops for values, vision, and strategies and provides feedback loops to show where the team or organization is and is not aligned.

PULL POWER

When we start with respect, we create pull through circles of influence. RTI leverages four elements to create pull:

- Purpose that pulls (values, vision)
- People who pull (transformers)
- Principles that pull (respect, trust, influence)
- Process that pulls (leaders of leaders)

The first step in the Influence sequence is to *honor bound-aries*. Honoring boundaries serves as a hinge between trust and influence because it brings together all the elements of respect and trust that optimize results and relationships. Honoring boundaries also determines which leadership and communication styles will be rewarded and reinforced in the culture.

Inappropriate aggressiveness does not honor boundaries and creates a push-push, whereas appropriate assertiveness honors boundaries through *simultaneous* respect, which leads to trust and sustainable influence. Assertiveness also spits disrespect out of the system and pulls capable leaders into the team or organization, much like the gravity of the sun pulls the planets into their orbits. This enables us to attract, create, and develop more leaders. A memorable proposition for expressing this boundary balance is this aphorism: *say and do what you mean, but don't be mean.*

The second step in the Influence sequence is to *create leaders.* When leaders view their role as creating more leaders, not simply leading or managing followers, it transforms their teams and organizations. At this point, the goal and output of the full RTI sequence comes to fruition: to establish a leaders-of-leaders culture to attract, keep, develop, align, and promote leaders to grow, produce, and reproduce in a sustainable system that is always ready to lead change. A quote adapted from Gandhi articulates this concept: "The measure of you as a leader isn't how many followers you have but how many leaders you create."

Say and do what you mean, but don't be mean.

HONOR BOUNDARIES

RESPECT ❯	TRUST ❯	INFLUENCE
SUSPEND ASSUMPTIONS	CULTIVATE OPENNESS	HONOR BOUNDARIES
VALUE DIFFERENCES	EXPAND DIALOGUE	CREATE LEADERS

While openness and possibility thinking are crucial mindsets for solving problems and developing change capability, all team members are entitled to set a limit to their degree of personal openness and to set their own boundaries.

This is especially true when we are trying to get people to adopt change. We can't simply push change on others, crossing their boundaries without consequences.

Once you see how boundaries relate to influence, you will know how important setting boundaries is to creating a respect culture.

Boundaries are the nexus of respect and trust. Boundaries determine whether you cross the line into influence or manipulation. When you respect boundaries, you build trust and pull with influence. When you disrespect boundaries, you destroy trust and must resort to pushing, manipulation, or control.

> Boundaries determine whether you cross
> the line into influence or manipulation.

When leaders choose the RTI path, they seek to honor and respect boundaries as a guide to every action they take. Respecting boundaries becomes the principled and pragmatic way they approach change, differentiate influence from control, hold people accountable, and optimize both results and relationships.

Boundaries are like property lines that distinguish an individual's identity from others in relation to choices, responsibilities, and limits. My identity should not be wrapped up in you, and your identity should not be wrapped up in me. We should have our own boundaries (space) and our own identities. We don't want to be in other people's space inappropriately, and people should not infringe on our space. That's when we cross the line.

FOUR TYPES OF BOUNDARIES

Researchers have identified four common types of boundaries, and I often see them play out within teams and organizations:

- Passive (or Submissive)
- Aggressive
- Passive-Aggressive
- Assertive

PASSIVE

People with passive boundaries tend to refrain from communicating their thoughts and feelings or advocating for their needs and wants. A passive boundary is like no boundary. It is like a yard with no fence. Your yard is my yard. Walk across my yard. Ride your bike across my yard. Walk your dog and let him do his thing in my yard. People with a passive boundary are unable to say, "Not in my yard!" While they may not want others to walk across their yard and are likely to feel frustrated or upset when they do, they are unable to share those feelings with the trespasser. Their thought pattern is "I'm not okay, but you are ok." They will repress their feelings and avoid confrontations. The passive boundary consistently results in "I lose, and everyone else wins."

Passive people tend to accept change readily, even when they don't agree with or believe in it, simply to not rock the boat. But they don't actively engage as change champions. It's enrollment rather than commitment.

AGGRESSIVE

People with aggressive boundaries put up a wall with a large sign that says, "Stay out of my yard. You are not welcome here. Beware of the dog!" When people with aggressive boundaries encounter somebody else's wall, they might try to knock it down. They relish the competition. They express their thoughts and feelings and advocate for their needs and wants at the expense of others. They don't care what others think. They may even use the cloak of authenticity as their excuse: "I just say what I think. You always know exactly where I'm coming from." However, this is simply an *excuse* to say what they mean, even if it's mean.

The aggressive boundary thought pattern is "I'm okay, but you are not okay. I respect myself. I don't respect you. I'm going to tell you tell you exactly what I think, even if it's disrespectful."

The behavior is attack-like. And it surfaces with the people they work with and live with, not just with competitors. People with an aggressive boundary are focused on achieving their goals even if they must dominate and overpower others to reach them. They climb the ladder of success by pushing everyone else off the rungs. The result is that they win, and others lose. Obviously, this result is not optimal. Even if they appear to be successful at times, relationships inevitably become rocky. The behavior *always* backfires at some point.

Aggressive leaders tend to push change on others, which creates a push-push dynamic, escalating resistance. And even if the intent is noble or the change is positive, the aggressive approach still has a negative impact. It isn't sustainable over time. Since aggressive people don't prioritize respect, the *what* is more important than the *how*. It becomes more about loyalty, politics, fear, and intimidation to conform rather than influencing others to transform.

PASSIVE-AGGRESSIVE

The passive-aggressive boundary is like a road that looks safe to cross, but when you least expect it, a truck comes barreling toward you. This boundary exhibits temporary respect for self and a disguised lack of respect for others. It withholds thoughts, feelings, needs, and wants—then overstates them to the surprise and detriment of others.

People who possess this boundary often start with good intent. "I'm a nice person . . . until you tick me off." The problem is that I don't know when you'll get mad or if someone else made you mad before I entered the room. Regardless of intent, the people with passive-aggressive boundaries will eventually lose the respect, trust, and influence of their colleagues. It's like the *Peanuts* cartoon where Lucy persuades Charlie Brown to trust her to hold the football again for him to try to kick. Then Lucy jerks away the ball, and Charlie Brown tumbles to the ground again, to his chagrin. In the workplace, Charlie Brown will learn his lesson and find someone he trusts to hold the football.

The passive-aggressive thought pattern is "I'm not okay, but you are okay," and then it unexpectedly flips to "I'm okay, but you are not okay." The behavior that is generated by passive-aggressive feelings is repression followed by obses-sion. After being repressed for a while, the obsession becomes quite intense and different from the messages previously sent. Because of this incongruence, it's difficult to trust a person with passive-aggressive boundaries. Passive-aggressive behav-ior is indicated first by avoidance and then by attack. This throws colleagues off and damages trust. The result is that the passive-aggressive person will lose and then turn around and make you lose. This is the worst result of all—and again, it often comes from a good intent to be more balanced! This is another perfect example of intent versus impact.

When it comes to change, you can never easily tell if a passive-aggressive person is a resister or not. They may appear to adopt change in a meeting but resist the same change in the grapevine, especially if the change impacts their world. When you're leading change, passive-aggressive people are very difficult.

ASSERTIVE

People with assertive boundaries show respect for both self and others *simultaneously*. If it's not simultaneous, it will be perceived as passive-aggressive or aggressive-passive. When we are assertive, we make direct statements of our thoughts, feelings, needs, and wants while respecting the thoughts, feelings, needs, and wants of others. This boundary is like a gate that represents reciprocal respect. You can knock on the gate. I can open the gate. You can't just walk into my yard without permission. There is mutual respect and reciprocal trust coming and going, in and out.

> People with assertive boundaries show respect for both self and others *simultaneously*.

The assertive thought pattern is: "I'm okay; you're okay. With this assertive boundary, we can value our differences. I don't have to agree with you, but I can respectfully listen to your point of view." Feelings are not repressed or obsessed. People with assertive boundaries can appropriately express how they are thinking and feeling. They make direct statements about their thoughts, feelings, needs, and wants. And since I'm okay and you're okay, it's okay for you to give me some feedback. I might not agree with it, but I am open to your feedback.

The result is win-win or no deal. Sometimes we may opt for no deal—a viable, assertive option.

Many people mistakenly or unintentionally use the terms *assertive* and *aggressive* interchangeably. Being assertive is not being aggressive. You can be too aggressive, and it will ultimately backfire in any relationship. But you can't be too assertive, if assertive means showing respect for you and the other person simultaneously. Being more assertive will only make the relationship better!

Leaders in healthy cultures set assertive boundaries. In effect, these leaders are saying, "We are not going to put up with passive behavior, aggressive behavior, or passive-aggressive behavior." If their behavior doesn't match this norm, a person may say, "Well, that's who I am." And the assertive leader can respond, "Well, if that's the way you are, then you need to change your behavior to align with our culture of respect. If you don't change, we need to talk about our options." That's honoring boundaries and being assertive about respect!

Leaders in healthy cultures set assertive boundaries.

When leading change, assertive leaders create pull and engagement, or there is no deal. Aggressive leaders create push, which backfires into push-push and lose-lose resistance.

Since boundaries are often intangible, I created this chart to help leaders understand the four different boundaries and how they impact people's thoughts, feelings, behaviors, and results.

ESTABLISHING AND HONORING ACCEPTABLE BOUNDARIES

	PASSIVE	AGGRESSIVE	PASSIVE AGGRESSIVE	ASSERTIVE
BOUNDARIES	Yard	Wall	Road	Gate
THOUGHTS	You're OK I'm Not OK	You're Not OK I'm OK	I'm Not OK You're Not OK	I'm OK You're OK
FEELINGS	Repression	Obsession	Repression then Obsession	Expression and Feedback
BEHAVIORS	Avoid	Attack	Avoid then Attack	Confront and Resolve
RESULTS	Lose/Win	Win/Lose	Lose/Lose	Win/Win or No Deal

People establish boundaries based on past experiences. The boundaries we had growing up in our families tend to remain in place unless we purposefully change them. In teams and organizations, boundary issues are likely to surface because you are bringing together individuals with different backgrounds and experiences.

Boundaries are the borders between trust and influence. Respecting boundaries builds trust and positive influence. When leaders create clear boundaries, they show respect for themselves and others. Appropriate boundaries build credibility and influence, regardless of your position in life or work. You will increase positive, sustainable influence when you set and honor appropriate boundaries.

> Appropriate boundaries build credibility and influence, regardless of your position in life or work.

The measure of you as a leader isn't how many followers you have but how many leaders you create.

CREATE LEADERS

RESPECT ⊘	TRUST ⊘	INFLUENCE
SUSPEND ASSUMPTIONS	CULTIVATE OPENNESS	HONOR BOUNDARIES
VALUE DIFFERENCES	EXPAND DIALOGUE	CREATE LEADERS

Let's imagine that an organization is working hard to put all the respect, trust, and influence pieces into place. They have built a culture that suspends assumptions and values differences. Leaders have set the tone for cultivating openness and expanding dialogue. They are well on their way to honoring boundaries. How can the RTI system still go sideways?

When an organization fails to create leaders at all levels, change initiatives and the RTI system as a whole will inevitably fail to take hold. For the RTI system to work, organizations need to vanquish the old paradigm of a few top executives in corner offices calling all the shots. A command-and-control culture stifles innovation, creativity, and collaboration. In organizations where people do only what they're told to do and are rewarded for doing what they are told, the RTI system and major change initiatives are doomed.

This last piece of the RTI model is designed to underscore the importance of creating leaders up and down the organization. I'm not talking about positional leadership that comes with titles and managerial spots on an org chart. I'm talking about personal leadership and mindset leadership.

> A change-ready organization is
> proactively and purposefully structured
> around creating leaders.

SOURCE AND FORCE

A change-ready organization is proactively and purposefully structured around creating leaders. It establishes and supports a culture that attracts, keeps, and develops leaders. It aligns and promotes leadership as a catalyst for transformation. This structure facilitates a dynamic force that generates influence and innovation, as opposed to a coercive force that generates uniformity and conformity. The right structure allows energy to flow to the path of least resistance. Like the sun, this structure generates energy from its core and influences outward to the other parts of the system. Likewise, the influence of a leader emanates from core principles and mindset.

SIX R'S OF CREATING A LEADERSHIP CULTURE

To create a leadership culture and nurture change capability, leaders need to focus on six R's:

1. Recruit the right people, especially leaders.
2. Reward the right behaviors and mindsets.
3. Retain the right people, especially leaders.

4. Retrain as you're making changes that require new capabilities.
5. Reposition people who are not in the right position.
6. Replace people who resist desired change or don't align with the culture.

The two most important leverage points are *recruit* and *replace*. If you lack the wisdom to recruit and the courage to replace, you will have minimal change capability.

Most organizations don't regularly replace habitual slackers and high resisters because they don't recruit the right leaders. This makes *recruit* the top leverage point since bad recruiting keeps us from replacing difficult people. Turnover is expensive, disruptive, and time-consuming. It's easier to be passive and keep the people you have. But if you're not replacing problematic people, you're making it harder on everybody else. You're not doing anybody any favors. In fact, you're limiting the organization's change capability and thus stunting its growth and performance. And most of all, you lose the best leaders as they get tired of dealing with slackers. You won't have a culture that attracts leaders.

This is where the assertive boundary generates influence. By being assertive, you create a culture that attracts the best leaders.

> By being assertive, you create a culture
> that attracts the best leaders.

LEADERSHIP AS INFLUENCE

Leadership has many meanings and associations. For example, it is linked to vision, management, title, position, personality, and charisma. In his book *Leadership: Strategies for Taking Charge*, Warren Bennis offers a simple definition: "Leadership is turning intention into reality." This definition directly or indirectly covers most elements of effective leadership.

I believe we can sum up leadership in one word: *influence.* We tend to think of leadership as something practiced by people who are called "leaders" by virtue of holding some office or position. However, when we think about leadership as influence, we expand the scope beyond positional leadership to include personal leadership as well. If you are influencing colleagues, customers, or partners every day, then you are exercising personal leadership.

When leaders create leaders, they become transformers who are also leading within and beyond their circles of influence. As you think about leadership as influence, consider your circles of influence at work. For example, you might have a management circle, team circle, project circle, volunteer circle, social circle, and customer support circle. In each circle, you influence several people. You may be amazed to see how many people fall into your direct circle of influence every day!

Now think about the ripple effect of our circle of influence. Each person we influence in turn influences other people. Our actions have a ripple effect within and outside our circles. Each one of us, directly and indirectly, influences dozens of people every day, and our circles of influence can have a profound influence, for better or for worse, on transformational change.

OVER-MANAGED AND UNDER-LED

A leadership culture—or what I call a leaders-of-leaders culture—builds change capability and capacity. This culture—and a support system to sustain it in both a personal and positional leadership capacity—is the optimal strategy.

In his book *Leading Change*, John Kotter states that most change initiatives are over-managed and under-led. He shows that complex change requires 10 to 30 percent management skills and 70 to 90 percent leadership skills. Yes, managing change is important, but leading change is imperative. Since policies and procedures can't cover every context in a complex change situation, leaders at all levels must have the freedom to make decisions based on the real-time moments of truth in front of them. They also must know when a well-intended policy backfires in a situation and discern when a procedure is counterproductive.

> Managing change is important,
> but leading change is imperative.

TOP-LINE TO FRONT-LINE CONGRUENCY

A leadership culture generates broad-based leadership capability and capacity from the top line to the front line. In fact, front-line leadership is as important as top-line leadership in implementing change. If you don't have competent leadership on the front line, you can't implement or sustain the change. In other words, we aren't looking for truck drivers; we are looking to hire leaders who happen to drive a truck, and hopefully enjoy driving a truck. We aren't hiring receptionists; we are hiring leaders who have the skills of a receptionist, and hopefully enjoy being a receptionist. This leadership mindset makes an enormous difference.

> A leadership culture generates
> broad-based leadership capability and
> capacity from the top line to the front line.

WILL THE TRUCK DRIVER GET IT?

When working with organizations, I require front-line leaders to have a prominent presence at the start of any change initiative. I purposefully seek their input and influence. *Those who implement should have input.* This broad-based leadership point of view goes against the cultural grain in many hierarchical organizations. For example, I once suggested that a truck driver be present at a change initiative meeting. The CEO challenged me. "Will the truck driver get it?" Since I knew this CEO quite well, I replied, "Yes, probably better than you or any other executive in this room gets it."

With a smile and a surprised look, he asked, "How's that?"

I replied, "Because most of the issues we will be addressing are being done *to* the truck drivers. Trust me, they not only get it; they *feel* it."

After the session, the CEO said, "You were right! The most insightful input came from the truck driver." This driver was a leader, a transformer, who happened to drive a truck.

TAMMY TO THE RESCUE

Tammy had been a bartender when she was hired at Arbor Material Handling as a service dispatcher. She soon took on the role of warranty administrator. Both were task-oriented functions with no formal leadership position or authority. However, I and the leadership team soon realized that Tammy wielded influence that outmatched her title. Her influence stemmed from her capabilities and relationships.

As part of a change capability initiative I was facilitating at Arbor, we required a front-line person to be on the first transformer team. Tammy quickly distinguished herself as a diligent and trustworthy worker who could get the job done, so the CEO thought Tammy would be a good fit for this role on the transformer team.

Tammy delivered beyond everyone's expectations. The transformer team quickly noticed that she had some of the most insightful input. She articulated the front-line perspective clearly and concisely. She thrived in this new team environment where she could be herself—authentic, honest, and assertive. Her comfort level with the group and her personal confidence grew exponentially over a short period of time.

At a critical point in the culture transformation that we had initiated, the leadership team discovered a pocket of resistance from a manager at a key branch. He had claimed to be a solid supporter of the change, but the hidden resistance that we uncovered threatened the entire transformation. It was critical that we address the problem quickly to keep the momentum going. The leadership team needed to replace this manager with someone who had internal knowledge, could lead a quick turnaround, and modeled the new culture they desired.

As the leadership discussed who could intervene and lead this turnaround, Tammy's name surfaced. Tammy's experience on the transformer team had given her a platform to be noticed. In a coaching session, she shared with me that the role of branch manager exceeded her career aspirations. She was nervous about the promotional leap, but she eventually mustered the confidence to accept the challenge.

In just a few months, Tammy rose from an individual contributor to a courageous leader the company depended on to fix a badly broken branch in a growing market that was critical to the company's growth and success. The pressure on Tammy to succeed was intense, and the promotion was a stretch for her. But she rose to the occasion with coaching and support from the other transformer team members.

The nexus of Tammy's discipline and diligence and the respect and trust culture created new capacity from an otherwise unnoticed source of leadership at just the right time. Arbor learned to reproduce this situation over and over, and Tammy was the perfect prototype that got the leaders-of-leaders ball rolling.

CLOSE TO THE ACTION

Front-line leaders are closer to the action and have key information that top-line leaders can't access easily or consistently. This information must be absorbed, prioritized, and communicated to the mid-line and top line accurately and clearly for optimal decision-making and problem-solving.

Critical information is at the mercy of the discernment of the front-line leaders. Technology has made some just-in-time information easier, but it can't always replace boots-on-the-ground information where nuances are critical for making wise decisions. Much of the information needed is subjective and fluid.

MODELING TRANSFORMATIONAL CHANGE

Leaders must model the transformational change that they hope to achieve. They can't simply present a strategy and hope people will let go of the past and reach toward the future. People must see the change modeled by their leaders. Modeling is the essence of integrity and builds credibility and trust for the leader as well as the change process. If leaders do not make personal transformations, how can they expect the people on their team to make such transformations?

WHAT A LEADERS-OF-LEADERS CULTURE LOOKS LIKE

What does a leaders-of-leaders culture look like?

When those who lack the title of leader start viewing themselves as leaders, it changes everything. When leaders view their role as creating leaders, not simply leading or managing followers, it transforms their teams and organizations. This paradigm shift changes the behavior of both non-positional leaders and positional leaders.

> When those who lack the title of leader start viewing themselves as leaders, it changes everything.

RESPECT OR ELSE!

One day I received an out-of-the-blue email from my former client Scott. I had coached Scott when he was promoted from a twenty-something sales superstar to a new sales manager. It was a challenging transition for him, but he was able pull it off due to his leadership qualities, impeccable discipline, and openness to coaching.

During the time I had lost touch with Scott, he was hired as the CEO of the most successful dealership in the Raymond Materials Handling system. Scott had decided he couldn't take the dealership to the next level with the existing culture. He engaged me to help him transform the dealership from a command-and-control culture to a leaders-of-leaders system anchored in respect.

Scott and his leadership team were facing a particular culture problem. After beginning to implement a "customer first" system, some employees learned they could use the sword of disrespect against fellow employees in the name of "customer first." The system had backfired. Scott and his leadership team changed their DNA statement to: "Always keep the customer #1, both internal *and* external." Another point in their DNA statement reminded employees that they were striving to "develop a leaders-of-leaders culture grounded in respect, trust, and positive influence."

At a crucial tipping point in their transition, Scott came face-to-face with a difficult decision. His top salesperson blatantly and publicly disrespected another employee. The salesperson assumed from previous experience that he would not be held accountable due to his sales numbers and prowess. If Scott and the leadership team didn't hold this salesperson accountable, however, it would send the message that they weren't committed to the *Start with Respect* culture. Scott called his team together to discuss this situation and its consequences. With the support of his team, Scott decided to fire this salesperson. Yes, they feared losing sales, but they stood firm, knowing that they needed to prove they were serious about building a culture of respect. Everyone in the organization, no matter their contribution, needed to be on board or find the door.

Employees were on edge about what Scott would do. When he made the tough call, you could feel a collective sense of relief and applause from every corner of the company. They wanted the new respect culture to take root. They didn't want to go back to their old ways. Their fears of losing sales never materialized. In fact, they ended up gaining sales because the morale of the other salespeople and employees rose to an all-time high. Scott and his team had made the right call, and respect took root as a foundation of their new, leaders-of-leaders culture.

A PEOPLE-FIRST MINDSET

You can't manage change like a project and expect sustainable results. You must lead change. You must focus on people, first and foremost. This is why the measure of you as a leader isn't how many followers you have but how many leaders you create. And when you create more leaders, you become more change capable.

The leader's mindset influences everything about the change process—the structure, expectations, and selection of team members. It all flows from the leader's mindset and level of emotional intelligence. The system *always* arises from the mindset of the leader!

Interested in diving deeper into Influence?
Download more resources and tools at
startwithrespect.com.

Make the right thing to do the path of least resistance.

SUSTAINABLE CHANGE AND SYSTEMS THINKING

RESPECT >	TRUST >	INFLUENCE
SUSPEND ASSUMPTIONS	CULTIVATE OPENNESS	HONOR BOUNDARIES
VALUE DIFFERENCES	EXPAND DIALOGUE	CREATE LEADERS

"Impossible!"

"You're crazy!"

"Good luck with that!"

When Tim Koval was appointed CEO of Arbor Material Handling, he was told by several people that he was fighting an unwinnable battle. Tim arrived after his company acquired Arbor and found a business that was only marginally successful. Even more concerning, this materials handling and intralogistics dealership with operations in three Northeast states was plagued by an unhealthy culture. Tim soon discovered poor communication and a lack of accountability, both within and between departments. Sales hated service. Service hated sales. Everybody hated rentals and parts.

Tim faced a complicated context and more problems than imaginable. For example, two of the most seriously mismanaged departments were led by nephews of the former owner, who was the younger brother of a former senior executive at Tim's employer—the acquiring company. The odds were not in Tim's favor!

A few advisers urged Tim to wipe the slate clean—to fire the whole leadership team and start over. While that radical move was tempting, Tim chose to transform the system by starting with respect. Some leaders didn't make the journey because they couldn't change their mindset, but others transformed and thrived. Despite the upfront challenges, it was one of the most successful transformations I've ever witnessed.

Tim led a cultural transformation from disrespect to respect, from command-and-control to leaders of leaders, from bunkered silos to cross-functional and multi-level collaboration, from fear and politics to open dialogue, from "my department first" thinking to systems thinking. Arbor's employees became relentlessly focused on generating win-win solutions while optimizing both internal and external relationships. People came to understand that there could be no personal or departmental success unless there was customer and company success. Customer and company success could only be achieved if everyone's viewpoints and concerns were understood, respected, and considered.

Tim put it this way: "Respect, trust, and influence played a vital role in helping us double our revenue by providing a system to transform our culture, develop leaders, increase company-wide collaboration, and improve our processes and operations."

Over Tim's tenure, Arbor was able to grow revenue at a compounded annual growth rate of more than 15 percent while increasing profitability at an even faster pace.

Tim and his transformer team created an ARBOR acrostic to articulate the vision of their new system: Achieving Results By Optimizing Relationships. This attracted high-quality employees like a magnet. Arbor transformed from a toxic workplace to the envy of their competitors. By the time Tim retired, he had set Arbor up for a bright future.

But could Arbor's leaders sustain the outstanding system they inherited?

Tim understood the power of integrating unchanging principles and systems thinking into Arbor so that the transformation would last long after he departed the company. This chapter focuses on the power of such systems thinking and sustainability.

PATH OF LEAST RESISTANCE

In his book *The Path of Least Resistance*, Robert Fritz explains that "structure determines behavior" and describes its route as "the path of least resistance," similar to the way water flows. Fritz advocates for making the *right* thing to do the *easiest* thing to do.

When creating a respect-based system, we want respect to be the easiest thing to do, the path of least resistance.

Organizational systems are held captive by the mindset of their leaders. The efficacy of the system is always born out of the prevailing mindset of its leaders. A respect mindset will lead to a respect-based system, as long as the leaders can also understand and support the system.

> Organizational systems are held captive
> by the mindset of their leaders.

HOW NOT TO FIX A JERK

In his book *The Fifth Discipline*, MIT professor and systems expert Peter Senge notes that systems are so powerful that "when placed in the same system, people, no matter how different, tend to produce similar results." This explains why even the best leaders may fail to make meaningful changes in organizations with suboptimal systems. They become stuck, stymied, and discouraged. They often leave in search of a healthier organization and better culture where they can lead at their best. These are the leaders we need most for transformational change—they are transformers! And yet our structures and cultures often drive transformers away. Strong leaders often leave organizations because of suboptimal systems.

Our first step in creating a better system is to ensure our structure and culture are congruent with our intentions. Remember Warren Bennis's definition of leadership: turning intentions into reality. *It's usually the lack of systems thinking that keeps our intentions from becoming reality!* For example, we can't create a culture of respect if our system rewards disrespect. We can't send the jerk boss off to training and think that will fix the system. After attending his HR-ordered conflict-resolution seminar, the jerk might be under the illusion that he's changed. Most likely he's changed his techniques but not his mindset. And the organization has not addressed the larger systemic change that is needed to assure that the jerk's behaviors are not acceptable in a respect-based culture.

WE'RE LIKE KIDS AT CAMP

During my first career as a high school English teacher and coach, I ran educational sports camps during the summers. I would regularly meet and greet campers who practiced risky behaviors. At home they had been in serious trouble or had struggled with addictions. At camp, the other counselors and I worked hard to keep them away from negative forces. We taught them how to make better choices.

During camp week, they got away from their broken family systems, old friends, and familiar patterns. They made new friends, practiced making better decisions, and became more proactive and positive. They developed good intentions to change for the better.

And then it was time for them to go home. They had changed, but the system back home had not changed. Even though it was unhealthy, it was familiar and provided them a perverted sense of emotional security. Sadly, several of these kids reverted to old behaviors that produced results like the ones of the past. Such backtracking is not limited to high-risk kids. When returning to a broken system, adults will also fall back into old mindsets and social networks, making it easier for them to return to familiar habits and dysfunctional behaviors.

FOUR COMMON SYSTEM RESPONSES

Over the years, I have observed that people tend to have four common responses to systems:

1. **Live with the system**. This first response resembles a defeatist attitude: "I can't do anything about it. I'll just go along to get along. No use rocking the boat. My voice doesn't matter. The jerks running this thing won't listen to me. I'll put in my time and collect my paycheck. If something better comes along, I'm out of here."

2. **Beat the system**. The second response is to push against the system and try to beat it. Inevitably, the system will push back until it beats you to a pulp. The harder you push against a system, the harder it pushes back. Sooner or later, those who try to beat the system realize their battle is in vain and either give it up or get booted out.

> The harder you push against a system,
> the harder it pushes back.

3. **Go around the system**. These people are dedicated to meeting their goals and getting their job done. They think, "If the system isn't helping me, I'll go around it." They pursue workarounds with good intent—to get the sale or to serve the customer, for example. They may even be rewarded for going around the system in the name of being proactive and productive. However, in doing so, they often make the flawed system worse and create unaligned subsystems.

4. **Challenge and change the system**. When organizations have a system problem, the only way to fix it is for someone to step up and challenge the system. After the initial challenge, there must be momentum to create a new system that will replace the old system that isn't working. The optimal way to challenge and change a system is to have the capability to transition to a new system in an assertive and respectful manner and to optimize both results and relationships as a foundation of the new system.

WHAT YOU SEE MAY NOT BE WHAT'S HAPPENING

When problems surface in organizations, it is easy to spot surface-level behaviors that appear to be causing the issue. However, it is what's beneath the behavior—system, structure, culture, and mindsets—that's driving the behavior. And those core drivers are harder to spot.

Leaders can't fix a system they can't see. It's the unseen iceberg beneath the water that sinks the ship. Leaders must uncover how each part of the system impacts the whole. They must think differently about what is causing the problems they are encountering. They must learn how to see what's beneath the surface so that they can spot the iceberg.

Leaders can't fix a system they can't see.
It's the unseen iceberg beneath the
water that sinks the ship.

SEEING SYSTEMS WITH GAME EYES

I once had the pleasure of visiting a game reserve in South Africa with my business partners Dr. Greg Gray and his wife, Karen. During the day, our focus was on an instructional design project. At dusk and dawn, when the animals were active, we would ride through the game reserve.

Riding along, Greg pointed and said, "Check out that bird." I couldn't spot the bird.

"Bill," he said, "you've got to put on your game eyes."

He explained that you can't look directly at the bird because if your sight doesn't land right on it, you won't see it among the trees. And you can't look at the trees; you have to look *through* the trees and see shape and pattern changes. When I finally spotted the bird, I noticed that it had a big, beautiful long tail that was perfectly camouflaged.

Having game eyes is like having a relaxed focus or utilizing peripheral vision. Hunters obviously need good game eyes because they must distinguish between different shapes and patterns. They are not necessarily attempting to spot the game; they are looking for movement or changes in shapes and patterns.

If leaders are hoping to see the system problems that exist in their culture, company, or market, they need to develop the vision, knowledge, and skills that enable them to see through the trees. To see beyond specific situations and detrimental behavior, they need to look at the whole picture. They must pinpoint patterns and the breaks in patterns. They must see beyond the obvious.

Many challenges that arise during change efforts are camouflaged. The outward semblance misrepresents something, disguises something, or exploits the natural surroundings. Game eyes give you the insight to see through the obvious and the camouflage that limits optimal decision-making and problem-solving. This is especially important for uncertainty, disruption, or strategic planning.

> Game eyes give you the insight to see through the obvious and the camouflage that limits optimal decision-making and problem-solving.

AMANDA'S GAME EYES

I first got to know Amanda Moorhead when she attended a train-the-trainer session for my *Journey to Newland* change capability process. Amanda's job was to support the logistics and implementation of HR projects. I immediately wondered how Amanda would handle the people-centric nature of our process (a perfect example of flawed assumptions on my part since I didn't realize she was dealing with the people part of the logistics equation). Amanda immediately locked in and engaged at a level that wowed the other highly skilled participants in the room. Amanda later pioneered our process in the United States and transformed two of the most important regions in her company.

What differentiates Amanda as a successful leader in transformational change is her game eyes—her ability to see how patterns of mindset and behavior impact teams and organizations.

Here is one example of how she does it. In our sessions, every person involved in Amanda's group would identify their change mindset profile that's based on the characters in the

Journey to Newland story and the change mindset model I describe in chapter two. Amanda noted these profiles on an organizational chart. She could then see how the mindset of the leader at the top of the org chart impacted each team. She would continue this process downstream to the front line and note everyone's impact on the team. She then identified the best influencers to coach as a beachhead to transform the whole team.

She determined the team dynamic not only within a team but also between teams to develop better cross-functional collaboration. This was particularly helpful with the shipping team and the receiving team, who were not getting along. The positive change Amanda created through this process was so noticeable it created a buzz in the other regions. She then used this success to socialize the change initiative to the next region through a positive vibe in the grapevine. She would do this systematically until each region was transformed.

This process was so effective that I now use it as an activity to teach game eyes, a model to improve team dynamic and impact, and an important tool to transform teams and organizations.

TRIM TABS

To change systems more effectively, leaders must also learn how to identify the root causes, or trim tabs. Trim tabs are the small devices that create big leverage. On a boat, a trim tab is like a small rudder on a larger rudder that captains use to adjust and turn a huge ship. On an airplane, the trim tabs are tiny compared to the wings. The pilot uses trim tabs to control the plane in flight; if they aren't properly attended to, the plane will crash. Trim tabs are a perfect symbol for small actions that have big effects.

LOCKERS IN POLAND

I once had the pleasure of working in Poland with a large international company that was mired in a transformational change within two of their most successful manufacturing plants. The company's leaders were merging some functions between the two plants, and they were having a hard time getting the front-line employees engaged and invested in the changes.

They had listened to my suggestion of valuing differences by inviting a front-line, non-managerial transformer to a meeting that was mostly made up of managers. We were working through a process of starting with the vision, listing the limiting factors, and finding the trim tabs among those factors. Front-line acceptance was one of those limiting factors.

We kept running into brick walls as we discussed raises, promotions, and the other obvious solutions they *assumed* would help get the front-line employees on board with the plans. Becoming frustrated, they turned to me for coaching on how to solve the problem. I began by saying, "Those who implement should have input." Then, I simply turned and asked the front-line person what he felt his colleagues needed to accept the change. To everyone's surprise, he quietly replied, "Lockers."

I asked him to explain. He went on to remind everyone in the room that for years they had asked for lockers, but management consistently ignored their request. They didn't seem to understand how important they were to the front-line workers. "If you get them lockers," he explained, "it will prove that you are finally listening to them. Paying some attention to their needs and showing that you care will go a long way in winning them over. And it will help them get the job done better."

The company bought some used lockers from a school, and like a charm, the front-line workers started accepting and engaging in the change.

The trim tab in this situation was a small purchase that generated a huge result. The tangible trim tab was lockers. The real trim tab was respect. It was respect that brought a front-line, non-managerial worker into the room and compelled the managers to act on his input.

When leaders are able to spot the small action at the root of an issue that will have a big impact, they can intervene in the system. Trim tabs serve as leverage points in a system. If you focus on these trim tabs, you can make transformational change happen better and faster.

SYSTEM LEVERAGE POINTS

In her book *Thinking in Systems*, Donella Meadows identifies twelve leverage points of a system:

1. Power to transcend paradigms
2. Paradigm and mindset from which the system arises
3. Goal of the system
4. Power to add, change, evolve, or self-organize
5. Rules of the system
6. Structure of information flow
7. Gain around driving positive feedback loops
8. Strength of negative feedback loops
9. Length of delays, relative to the rate of system changes
10. Structure of material stock and flows
11. Size of buffers and other stabilizing stock
12. Constants, parameters, numbers

When trying to change a system, most leaders will do what feels natural and normal and focus on items four through twelve—items that are mostly tangible and easy to see. Most organizations are obsessed with number five (rules of the system) and number six (structure of information flow).

They are missing the real leverage points: one, two, and three.

When someone says, "We have a communication problem," you might ask, "What paradigm or mindset led to this communication problem?" When someone points out a technology issue, it might camouflage a dysfunctional team. If you think you have a training problem, you might discover that you really have a learning problem if your system doesn't make it a priority to hire and promote learners.

FOCUS ON THE LEVERAGE POINTS THAT MATTER MOST

Meadows postulates that if you deal with leverage point one, then issues with points two through twelve will be easier to resolve. And if you focus on the top three leverage points, the others will either go away or be mitigated or neutralized.

The *Start with Respect* system is built on the first three leverage points. Effective leaders use the RTI system to generate an attractive pull. When this pull is applied evenly to all participants, it creates alignment. Again, it starts with the pull of RTI coming from the mindset of those creating and leading the system. We must see the system for what it is, leverage the energy through the principles built into its structure, and keep walking on the RTI path to sustain change.

OPTIMAL SYSTEMS AND SUSTAINABILITY

Good systems don't focus on the normal and natural but on the optimal, the long term, the sustainable results—and the respect path can take us beyond the normal to the optimal:

- Instead of pushing harder, pull better.
- Instead of starting with trust to get trust, start with respect.
- Instead of rewarding ideas, reward openness.
- Instead of looking for solutions, create options.
- Instead of micromanaging, increase mutual accountability.
- Instead of demanding that others conform, help them transform.
- Instead of fixating on results, fix the process.
- Instead of managing change, lead change.
- Instead of looking for security, look for opportunity.
- Instead of focusing on results, focus on both results and relationships.
- Instead of focusing on plans and projects, focus on people.
- Instead of chasing change, leverage unchanging principles.
- Instead of hiring for skill set, hire for mindset, skill set, and character.
- Instead of managing managers, create leaders.

The massive changes we have faced in recent years will not stop. In fact, the speed and complexity of change will only increase at an exponential pace. Get ready and stay ready by creating and maintaining a healthy RTI system. It's the best way to build a sustainable change capability system for your team or organization.

Interested in diving deeper into Sustainable Change
and Systems Thinking?
Download more resources and tools at
startwithrespect.com.

FINISH WITH RESPECT

At the beginning of this book, I introduced you to my client Daryl Holt. After we worked together to address foundational trust challenges that could stifle creativity and execution using the RTI system, Daryl asked me to help him to create a principle-centered, change-capable, leadership-infused system that could respond to disruption and uncertainty and create transformational change at any moment.

At that time, Daryl's company primarily sold packaged video game products. However, the industry was changing. Digital distribution and online services were emerging. Facebook and others started expanding into gaming during the worst part of the 2008 recession, and most of their games were free to play. The age of mobile games and in-game transactions and services was on the immediate horizon. And creating high-quality, premium experiences was getting more and more expensive, complex, and daunting. For Daryl's company to keep its top spots in key categories, it had to change its business model and approach quickly while the market was in flux.

With Daryl's commitment to the RTI path, he was able to infuse change capability into his team, creating new leaders and capabilities to handle the new context: rapid technology advancements, online competitors, and shifting customer habits and expectations. The next challenge was guiding his workforce to transform to an always-on, live-service mindset in which releasing games on time was no longer the end of a project but the beginning of its next phase. Since they had built their change capability, they were able to see, seize, and create new opportunities.

Sessions on valuing differences led to better communication and collaboration across game teams and centralized technology and creative groups that boosted morale, prevented last-minute changes, improved quality, and reduced cost and scheduling overruns. RTI allowed them to seamlessly merge functions across studio locations and cultures following reorganization. They also harnessed their new change capability to upgrade technology components, create games for new business models, add customer upgrades and in-app options within games to create additional revenue, and move to mobile and digital platforms quickly, passing over many of their competitors. In short, they transformed the studio and continued to innovate by embracing change, elevating change capability, and empowering a culture of leaders of leaders. Many of those transformers, including Daryl, are still with the company today, assuming senior leadership roles and scanning for the next change on the horizon.

THE LEGACY OF RESPECT

Throughout this book, I share examples of real leaders who modeled the *Start with Respect* mindset. All three of these excellent leaders made a similar comment to me during our heart-to-heart debrief conversations: they were committed to do what was right and lead with respect no matter what the cost. They would be willing to be fired or quit in an instant for the cause of respect. Their priority was to live with a clear conscience, be authentic, optimize results and relationships, and be a model of respect for their families and employees.

By their courage and consistency, they committed to start with respect and *finish with respect*. Respect is now a part of their legacy.

Start with respect and finish with respect.

I had the honor to help them sail their boats through uncertain waters, against rough winds, and around rocky crags in the sea of change. They held on to the unchangeable principle of respect like valiant mariners as the storms of resistance tried to beat them to a pulp and spit them into the sea. There were some tough conversations and decisions, but they relied on respect as their compass. It guided them through the rough waters. They demonstrated the wisdom to choose and the courage to confront. They stayed consistent, built trust, and grew positive, broad-based influence in each of their respective organizations. I witnessed them overcome resistance, create change capability, and establish a sustainable leaders-of-leaders culture against the odds.

YOU CAN DO IT TOO!

Are you ready? Is your organization ready? Ready or not, the workplace and business challenges that will require transformational change are right around the corner. When they show up—or even before they show up—I encourage you to take the first steps down the RTI path. I hope you will choose to be a bright ray of light in our dark world of disrespect and polarization. I hope you will start with respect and finish with respect.

SOURCES

Many books and authors have informed this book. Some works from this list were directly quoted, and others simply influenced my own thinking. I'm grateful for their research and scholarship.

Arbinger Institute. *Leadership and Self-Deception.* Berrett-Koehler, 2018.

Bennis, Warren, and Burt Nanus. *Leaders: The Strategies of Taking Charge.* Harper & Row, 1986.

Bolton, Robert. *People Skills.* Simon & Schuster, 1986.

Bridges, William. *Managing Transitions: Making the Most of Change.* DaCapo, 2009.

Cloud, Henry, and John Townsend. *Boundaries: When to Say Yes, How to Say No to Take Control of Your Life.* Zondervan, 1992.

Covey, Stephen R. *The Seven Habits of Highly Effective People.* Simon & Schuster, 1989.

Dobbin, Frank, and Alexandra Kalev. "Why Diversity Initiatives Fail—And What Works Better." *Harvard Business Review,* July–August 2016.

Fritz, Robert. *The Path of Least Resistance: Learning to Become the Creative Force in Your Life.* Ballentine, 1989.

Gladwell, Malcolm. *The Tipping Point: How Little Things Can Make a Big Difference.* Little, Brown, 2002.

Goleman, Daniel. *Emotional Intelligence.* Bantam, 1995.

Isaacs, William. *Dialogue and the Art of Thinking Together.* Doubleday, 1999.

Johnson, David W. *Reaching Out: Interpersonal Effectiveness and Self-Actualization.* Simon & Schuster, 1993.

Kaner, Sam. *Facilitator's Guide to Participatory Decision-Making.* Jossey-Bass, 2014.

Kotter, John P. *Leading Change.* Harvard Business School Press, 1996.

Land, George T., and Beth Jarman. *Breakpoint and Beyond: Mastering the Future—Today.* HarperCollins, 1992.

McKay, Matthew, Martha Davis, and Patrick Fanning. *Messages: The Communication Skills Book.* New Harbinger, 1995.

Meadows, Donella. *Thinking in Systems.* Chelsea Green, 2008.

Pearson, Christine and Christine Porath. "The Price of Incivility," *Harvard Business Review*, February 2013.

Powell, John. *Why Am I Afraid to Tell You Who I Am? Insights Into Personal Growth.* Thomas More, 1969.

Schein, Edgar H. *Humble Inquiry: The Gentle Art of Asking Instead of Telling.* Berrett-Koehler, 2013.

Senge, Peter. *The Dance of Change: The Challenges of Sustaining Momentum in Learning Organizations.* Doubleday, 1999.

Senge, Peter. *The Fifth Discipline.* Doubleday, 2006.

Shelton, Ken. *Suppression of Expression: An Unintended Consequence of Top-Down Leadership.* Executive Excellence, 2020.

ACKNOWLEDGMENTS

Many thanks to some very special people who provided inspiration, motivation, and unwavering support when I needed it most along this writing journey: Sierra Ricci, Keith Moore, Jack Whitley, David Lopez, and Dan Darden.

Additional thanks to special clients and colleagues who supported me and who model and apply these principles: Kevin Henry, Daryl Holt, Dr. Don Addison, Dr. Janelle Ward, Dr. John Townsend, Ron Weaver, David Bennett, Tony Norwood, Amanda Moorhead, Joe Machicote, Bob Bruton, Pat Bolton, Mark Bolton, Tarek El-Kadi, Scott Chontos, Tim Koval, Angela Baur, and John Baur.

I would also like to thank Ken Shelton, my writing collaborator and editor, for his coaching, patience, and persistence. And thanks to Lisa Shannon, editor of my original book with Wiley, who also served as final editor, consultant, and coordinator of publishing logistics for this book.

And thanks to Brian Carroll, Dr. Ken Percy, Dr. Ksenia Petrushkina, Ricardo Wilson, and Ron Thompson for helping me transform my health and wellness so I can keep writing.

ABOUT THE AUTHOR

Bill Poole is CEO of J2N Global and works as a personal, team, and organizational consultant and coach. He is the author of the *Journey to Newland* book and training materials (published by Wiley). He frequently speaks on the topics of transformational change and principle-centered leadership.

Bill is an innovative pioneer in leadership and change solutions. His groundbreaking materials evolved from three decades of experience coaching leaders in business, education, and nonprofit organizations. His work with large organizations (Coca-Cola, EA SPORTS, Nike, IBM, Caterpillar, Bank of America, PulteGroup), companies in transition, and corporate mergers and acquisitions provides a solid foundation for his collaborative partnerships and creative processes for transformational change.

Bill's global network of J2N Global associates serve as translators, facilitators, coaches, and consultants who utilize his models and materials with many of the largest and most successful companies in the world. This global experience affords him a relevant understanding of diverse cultures and learning styles.

Bill's business experience and academic background in education, communication, psychology, philosophy, and religion provide insights for producing innovative processes with creative teaching approaches. He completed his M.A. in religion and began an Ed.D. in leadership development at Columbia International University, where he created the foundational designs for *Journey to Newland* (co-developed with Coke Consolidated).

J2N Global is based in Tampa, Florida, and relies on the experience and insight of an elite advisory board. To learn more about Bill and his work, visit startwithrespect.com or j2nglobal.com or email him at bill@j2nglobal.com.

START WITH RESPECT WORKSHOPS, COACHING, AND CONSULTING

By Bill Poole and J2N Global

ARE YOU LEADING CHANGE, OR IS CHANGE LEADING YOU?

Maybe you're a leader who wants to implement new ideas, integrate groups from an acquisition or merger, or transform your team or organizational culture to be more agile and innovative. Or maybe you're looking for a systemic approach and common language to help people adopt change and be the disrupters rather than the disrupted.

Whatever complex or strategic change you're leading, our workshops, coaching, and consulting are designed to teach your team how to *Lead Change ... by Starting with Respect.*

- Inspire change and overcome resistance with Respect + Trust = Influence
- Cultivate an open and authentic culture over fear and conformity
- Create broad-based engagement, ownership, and accountability
- Improve multicultural, cross-functional, multilevel team effectiveness
- Transform mindset and systems for sustainable change capability

Contact info@j2nglobal.com for more details.

NEED A SPEAKER?

Bill has spoken to diverse audiences worldwide for keynotes, conferences, retreats, workshops, and sales and leadership training. Some of his most popular topics are:

- Leading Change
- Change Capability
- Breakthrough Transformation
- Leadership Development
- Principle-Centered Leadership
- Building and Leading Teams
- Valuing Differences
- Trust and Integrity
- Systems Thinking
- Innovation and Productivity

Go to startwithrespect.com or j2nglobal.com for more details, or contact info@j2nglobal.com.

Made in the USA
Columbia, SC
24 November 2024